Numeracy ACTIVITIES

Plenary, Practical & Problem Solving

Afzal Ahmed
Honor Williams
George Wickham

NetworkEducationalPress Ltd

Numeracy Activities
Key stage 3

Published by Network Educational Press Ltd.
PO Box 635
Stafford
ST16 1BF
www.networkpress.co.uk

ISBN 1 85539 103 1

Layout by Neil Hawkins
Illustrations by Kerry Ingram
Printed by MPG Books Ltd., Bodmin, Cornwall.

First published 1999 by Philip Allan Publishers Limited

Authors

The authors are based at the Mathematics Centre, University College, Chichester, one of the country's leading centres for mathematics education. **Afzal Ahmed** is Professor of Mathematics Education and Director of the Mathematics Centre. **Honor Williams** is Reader in Mathematics Education and Director of Teacher Education. **George Wickham** is Senior Lecturer in Mathematics Education.

The authors work closely with teachers and pupils across the age range and have considerable experience in research and curriculum development. In writing this material, they have drawn on their experience in the UK and internationally.

The authors acknowledge the help provided by Dianne Harmer, Senior Lecturer in Mathematics Education, in helping to proof-read and check the mathematical content for accuracy.

About this publication

The key aim of this file is to help pupils improve their fluency with number and measures. The pack concentrates on teaching skills as well as on pupils' learning experiences. Once teachers become familiar with the content and the approach (see pages 1–7 for a detailed introduction) it should be possible to adapt the material for varying classroom needs. Used appropriately, the units should also inprove pupils' confidence in tackling word problems. Some *general* features and suggestions for the use of the material are outlined below. Each unit commences with *specific* operational guidance for teachers.

- Although activities involve individual and group work, whole-class discussions can enrich the outcomes. When possible, individuals and groups should be encouraged to explain their understanding of tasks, methods and approaches to the rest of the class.
- Teachers can extend or modify the content to suit their pupils' circumstances by choosing, for example, different units of measurements, number operations or materials and contexts.
- The activities are designed so that answers, scores and targets can be improved by repeating and practising.
- The use of language is vital for pupils to understand and master mathematical concepts. It is important for teachers to support pupils so that they can understand written language and express their ideas to others.
- In some units, the contexts used are taken from outside pupils' *immediate* interests. This is designed to enable them to generalise their knowledge to new situations.

The units in this resource file are rich in mental activities, real life problems, reasoning and problem-solving activities. The following grid indicates the links to Objectives from the Framework for Teaching Mathematics: Years 7, 8 and 9.

Objectives from the Framework for Teaching Mathematics Year 7 to Year 9		Unit 1	Unit 2	Unit 3	Unit 4	Unit 5	Unit 6	Unit 7	Unit 8	Unit 9
Using and Applying Mathematics to Solve Problems	Solve word problems and investigate in a range of contexts	◆		◆	◆		◆	◆		◆
	Identify the information necessary to solve a problem; represent problems mathematically in a variety of forms	◆		◆	◆		◆	◆		◆
	Break problems into smaller steps or tasks; choose and use efficient methods and resources			◆	◆		◆	◆		◆
	Present and interpret solutions, explaining and justifying methods, inferences and reasoning						◆	◆		
	Suggest extensions to problems, conjecture and generalize; identify exceptional cases or counter-examples	◆	◆			◆				◆
Numbers and the Number System	Understand and use decimal notation and place value; multiply and divide integers and decimals by powers of 10		◆							◆
	Compare and order decimals									◆
	Round numbers to a given number of places									◆
	Order, add, subtract, multiply and divide positive and negative numbers	◆	◆		◆	◆		◆		
	Recognise and use multiples, factors and primes; use tests of divisibility						◆	◆		
	Use fraction notation; recognize and use the equivalence of fractions and decimals								◆	
	Calculate fractions of quantities; add, subtract, multiply and divide fractions					◆				
	Recognise the equivalence of fractions, decimals and percentages; calculate percentages and use them to solve problems				◆					
	Understand the relationship between ratio and proportion to solve simple problems				◆					◆
Calculations	Consolidate understanding of the operations of multiplication and division, their relationship to each other and to addition and subtraction; know how to use the laws of arithmetic									◆
	Consolidate the rapid recall of number facts and use known facts to derive unknown facts		◆				◆	◆		
	Make and justify estimates and approximations (of numbers and calculations)			◆	◆					
	Carry out more complex calculations using the facilities on a calculator			◆	◆					◆

Objectives from the Framework for Teaching Mathematics Year 7 to Year 9		Unit 1	Unit 2	Unit 3	Unit 4	Unit 5	Unit 6	Unit 7	Unit 8	Unit 9
Algebra	Use letters and symbols and distinguish their different roles in algebra						◆	◆		◆
	Know that algebraic operations follow the same conventions and order as arithmetic operations; use index notation and the index laws						◆			
	Use formulae from mathematics and other subjects				◆					◆
	Generate and describe sequences						◆			
	Generate terms of a sequence using term-to-term and position-to-term definitions of the sequence, on paper and using ICT						◆			
	Find the nth term, justifying its form by referring to the context in which it was generated						◆			
Measures	Use units of measurements to measure, estimate, calculate and solve problems in a range of contexts; convert between metric units and know rough metric equivalents of common imperial measures			◆	◆	◆				
	Extend the range of measures used to angle measure and bearings, and compound measures			◆	◆					
Handling Data	Calculate statistics from data, using ICT as appropriate								◆	◆
	Construct graphs and diagrams to represent data									◆
	Interpret diagrams and graphs, and draw inferences	◆								◆
	Use the vocabulary of probability								◆	
	Use the probability scale; find and justify theoretical probabilities								◆	
	Collect and record experimental data, and estimate probabilities based on the data								◆	
	Compare experimental and theoretical probabilities								◆	

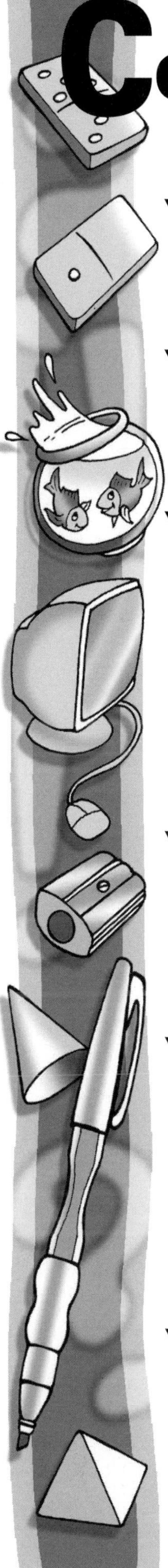

Contents

The mathematical activities in this file are designed to help pupils:

- gain communication skills – interpreting and expressing quantity, time and space
- understand relationships – describing, comparing, linking operations such as addition, subtraction, multiplication and division
- improve ability to cope with practical situations – shopping, planning, measuring accurately
- become systematic – ordering, tabulating, pattern-spotting, predicting, generalising
- improve mental tools – remembering, imagining, extending
- become curious – patterns , similarities, differences aid curiosity
- improve confidence in tackling tests

Introduction

Purpose

These materials have been prepared as a flexible resource to help teachers supplement their existing schemes of work. In order to provide a balanced mathematics curriculum and cope with the diversity in classrooms, teachers need to consider a wide range of factors when planning their schemes of work. Many of these are illustrated in the diagram below.

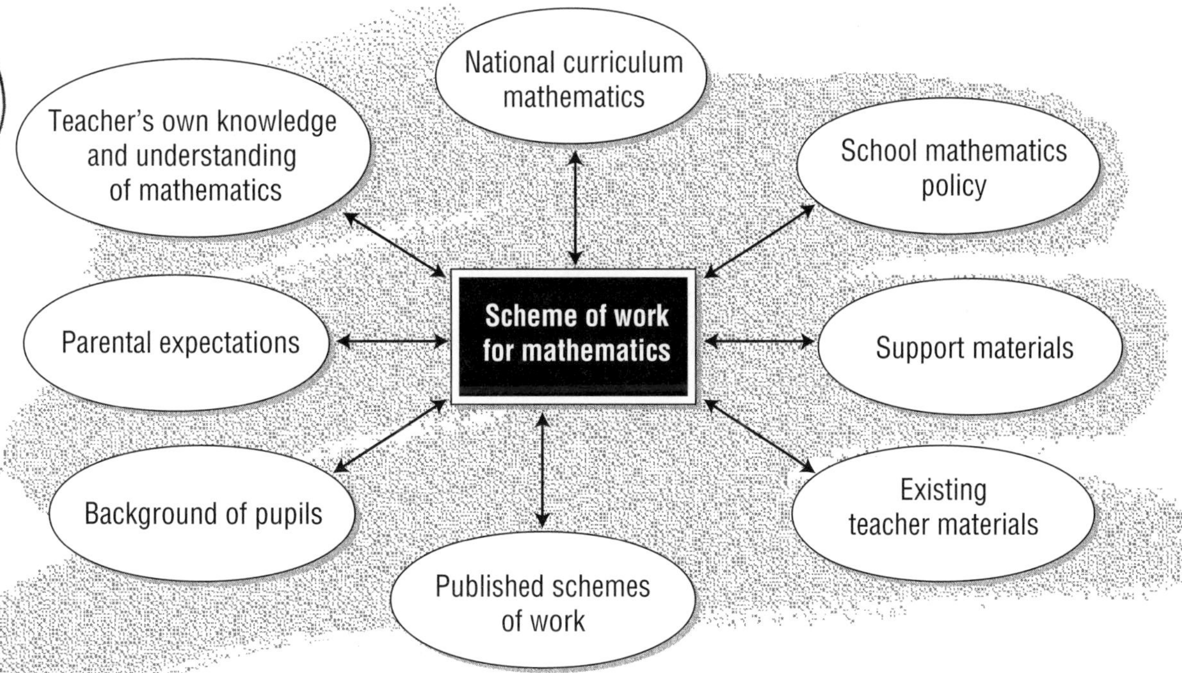

This support pack is arranged as a series of units with both teacher and pupil materials. The starting-points, questions and activities are designed to illustrate an approach that would involve pupils in appreciating and understanding the mathematical structures behind the tasks. This approach could easily be used to present other mathematics topics and content to suit particular ages and abilities. The material could also be used as homework tasks to be followed up in the classroom.

The pack focuses on aspects of numeracy concerned with number and measures. The importance of these skills and concepts as fundamental building blocks for further mathematical study cannot be overestimated and pupils should encounter these with increasing sophistication throughout their school life.

Measures The materials include activities that involve pupils in everyday practical and purposeful measuring activities. Estimation and approximation skills play an important role in developing pupils' measuring skills, and pupils talking about, recording and verifying their observations and assertions further aids their understanding.

Introduction

Number Developing pupils' understanding and confidence in formal written mathematical computations is a complex process. At Key Stage 3, it requires them to build on their range of experiences utilising concrete materials, mental strategies, pen and paper, and calculators. It is important that, having developed their own methods of calculating at an earlier stage, they can appreciate and use formal methods. The ability to determine whether a particular numerical solution is reasonable, verifying mental calculations, using tables, diagrams and graphs, deciding appropriate mathematical operations in particular contexts, etc., are vital experiences for becoming fluent with calculations and estimations. It is important to offer pupils opportunities for making connections between the various mathematical procedures they have learnt in order to solve new problems.

The units

All schools are engaged in the necessary but difficult task of adapting what they teach and how they teach to the wide-ranging abilities and interests of their pupils. The units in this pack are structured to meet, as far as possible, pupils' varying aptitudes and perspectives. They are designed to support teachers in a variety of ways and do not attempt to do the teachers' job for them. Each unit contains photocopiable pupil material on a main theme and each activity has the potential to be approached in a variety of ways. These activities can be modified to suit the needs of pupils while maintaining the main teaching and learning purposes. Each unit begins with outlining the main focus, content, notes for teachers, further activities, learning outcomes, evaluation and resources.

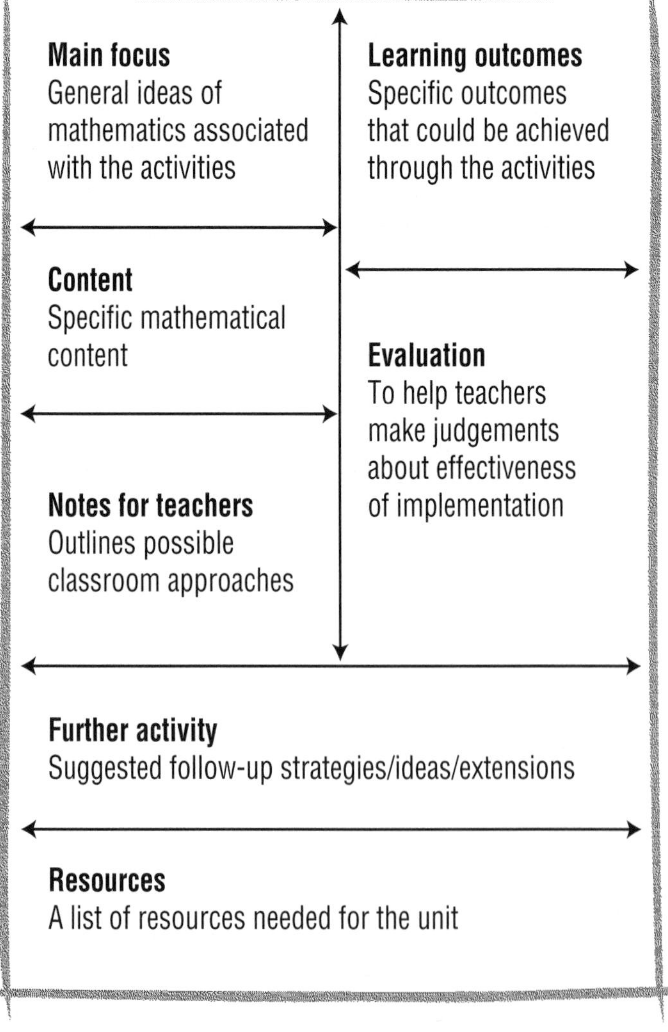

Main focus
General ideas of mathematics associated with the activities
Learning outcomes
Specific outcomes that could be achieved through the activities
Content
Specific mathematical content
Evaluation
To help teachers make judgements about effectiveness of implementation
Notes for teachers
Outlines possible classroom approaches
Further activity
Suggested follow-up strategies/ideas/extensions
Resources
A list of resources needed for the unit

The order of the units is not important. Teachers may wish to vary the order, depth and context of treatment of the units to suit the needs of their pupils.

Introduction

Teaching and learning assumptions

The units are based on the assumptions outlined below from the authors' considerable experience in curriculum development in mathematics.

Mathematics learning

Mathematics learning is more effective when it is interesting, enjoyable and challenging. In addition, the following assumptions about mathematical understanding have helped improve children's learning.

Mathematical understanding is improved when:

- pupils interact with people and manipulate materials in a wide variety of situations;
- pupils' experiences are used when appropriate as a source of learning activities;
- pupils are made aware of the relevance of mathematics to their lives;
- pupils are encouraged to use spoken and written language appropriate to their development in order to gain meaning from their mathematical experiences, for example to compose as well as solve problems;
- pupils are encouraged to describe and record relationships as well as to discover and create patterns;
- skills are sustained through meaningful practice and enjoyable drill – this also aids recall of facts and speed in computation;
- imaginative use is made of a wide variety of resources.

Talking, listening, reading and writing

For pupils to understand, apply and retain mathematics it is important for them to be engaged in talking, listening, reading and writing about mathematics. Language helps pupils to make their experiences meaningful. When they describe or write about their experiences or thinking, it helps them to clarify and develop their own understanding. Mathematical learning is enhanced by the appropriate use of language and, along with symbols and diagrams, it helps pupils formulate and express mathematical ideas.

Talking Providing opportunities for pupils to talk about mathematics is a very important step in helping them learn. Their experience is enriched by listening to their peers and teachers talk about mathematics. Through reflecting, justifying, verifying, questioning, etc., pupils are able to consolidate their understanding. Teachers' questions can sharpen pupils' thinking and also provide them with a model of how to use questioning to clarify and extend their own understanding. Spending time on discussing statements such as 'Is it true that 12% of £40 is the same as 40% of £12?' is crucial in enabling pupils to extract the correct mathematical operations required to solve problems stated in words.

Introduction

Mathematical symbols and terminology are a concise form of communication. Each symbol is packed with information that, when expressed in words, requires many words. It is also important to realise that one mathematical symbol may have several interpretations. For example:

14 – 9?	What is the difference between 14 and 9?	From 14 subtract 9
	14 take away 9	If I have 9, how many more do I need to make 14?
	Subtract 9 from 14	How many more than 9 is 14?
	What would you add to 9 to make 14?	What is 9 subtracted from 14?
		Take 9 from 14
	14 minus 9	How much bigger is 14 than 9?

When pupils are working from a textbook or task sheet and say '*We are stuck*', try asking them what they think the question or explanation means. Avoid your own explanations dominating pupils' mathematics. Think of questions you could ask to encourage pupils to extend their own line of thinking.

Listening Developing pupils' ability to listen to each other and to their teachers will help them in:

- decoding the mathematics from a situation;
- understanding key ideas;
- acquiring appropriate mathematical vocabulary;
- checking the relevance of their solutions to the original tasks.

By listening to pupils talking about mathematics, teachers can:

- gauge pupils' levels of understanding;
- ascertain pupils' difficulties, levels of confidence and attitudes towards mathematics;
- evaluate the effectiveness of their teaching approaches.

Providing mathematical activities that involve pupils in discussions is helpful for both teachers and pupils. It is important for pupils to have sufficient time to organise their thoughts and arrive at some conclusions. When pupils ask questions, teachers should try to resist offering information too quickly without determining pupils' understanding. For example, turn round some of the questions pupils ask you so that they can be involved in answering them.

Introduction

Reading How often do teachers hear comments such as: *'Is this an add or times sum?' 'This is too hard, I can't understand any of it.' 'What do I have to do here?'*

These comments arise because reading for mathematical meanings is not given a priority in the classroom. The difficulties in comprehending mathematical questions are only compounded when pupils' mathematical diet is dominated by activities that avoid words to compensate for real or apparent 'poor reading skills'.

In order to understand, apply and solve mathematical problems, we have to:

- read or listen to the problem;
- comprehend;
- select relevant data and information;
- translate the words into an appropriate mathematical form;
- carry out the necessary procedures;
- translate the answer back into the original context;
- consider if the answer is sensible.

Short cutting this process by only asking pupils to carry out set procedures inhibits mathematical learning.

Teachers can encourage pupils to read for mathematical meanings by using a variety of materials and strategies:

- inviting pupils to write about the mathematics they do and reading each others' work;
- asking pupils to make up questions around simple mathematical procedures for others to solve;
- asking pupils to decode instructions for model making and games;
- using everyday materials such as newspapers, posters or packaging.

Writing Writing and recording is a powerful means of reinforcing mathematical understanding. It helps pupils to:

- make their thinking explicit and clarify ideas;
- identify different pathways to solutions;
- develop mathematical notation.

It also helps teachers to:

- diagnose misconceptions;
- determine a basis for progressing to the next stage.

It is important that pupils are aware of the purpose for their writing, feel motivated and confident, and are comfortable in using their own words and language patterns. Try, for example, to avoid asking pupils simply to 'write it down'. Create a situation where writing becomes a necessary element for successful completion of the task.

Introduction

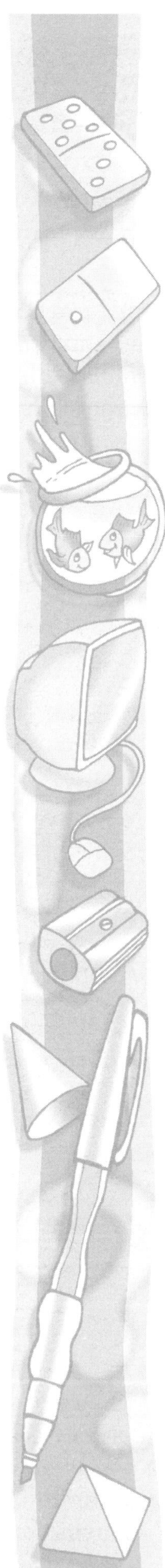

Some classroom strategies for developing talking, listening, reading and writing[1]

- Involve pupils in simple starting points, then try asking how they might vary these or what questions they could think up to answer next. Collect together pupils' suggestions for variations or questions, perhaps on the board or on a large sheet of paper, and try inviting them to follow up a suggestion of their choice.
- Ask pupils to keep a record of questions or other ideas they have not attempted. Encourage them to choose one of those questions to work at on appropriate occasions.
- Put up examples of pupils' own questions on display. Invite groups to look at and perhaps work on other groups' questions.
- Do not always give pupils rules that work; invite them to try some that do not and to explain why they do not.
- Encourage pupils to find methods and rules for themselves. Try to involve them in comparing the methods to agree on the most efficient. See if you can think of ways of involving pupils in generalising for themselves.
- When you want pupils to practise skills, think whether it would be possible for such practice to emerge through their own enquiries or problems that will necessitate the use of these skills.
- Think how you might 'twist' tasks and questions described in textbooks, task sheets or test papers so that pupils can become more involved in making decisions, describing patterns and relationships and testing conjectures.
- Help pupils to appreciate the importance of asking questions such as 'Is this sensible?', 'Can I check this for myself?' Offer activities that will involve pupils in decisions relating to the 'correctness' of a piece of mathematics.
- Show pupils examples of mistakes. Ask them to sort out what the mistakes are and to think how they might have arisen.
- Consider how you might incorporate the terms and notations that you want pupils to learn, so that meaning can be readily ascribed to them and they can be seen as helpful and necessary.
- Encourage pupils to look for connections between old and new situations, ideas and skills and to ask themselves whether something they did previously might be of use in solving their new problems.
- When a pupil comes up with something that appears initially to be off the track, try to stop yourself from immediately implying that this is the case. What about the possibility of it being kept as a 'further idea' for later?

[1] These strategies have been taken from Ahmed, A. and Williams, H. (1992) *The Raising Achievement in Mathematics Project Report*, WSIHE.

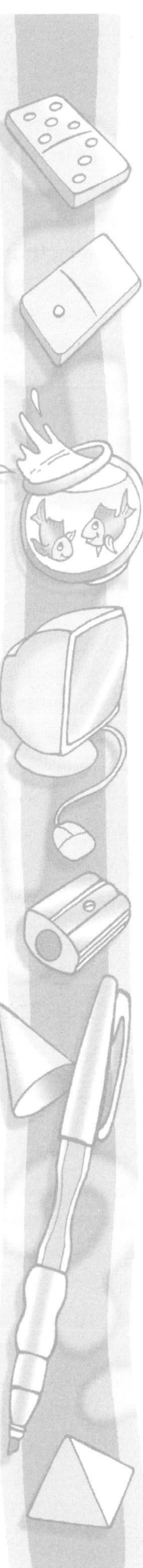

Introduction

The activities within the units of this resource pack provide considerable scope for teachers to utilise these strategies.

Learning outcomes

All teachers would wish their pupils to be challenged sufficiently for them to achieve to the best of their ability. The implication of this is that teachers should gain as much insight as possible into their pupils' needs, aptitudes and strengths. This will help in offering them appropriate mathematical tasks.

The following questions might prove helpful in evaluating general learning outcomes:

- ◆ Does the pupil know and understand what is required?
- ◆ Does the pupil need more experience with materials?
- ◆ Does the pupil need extension, consolidation or remediation in a particular area?
- ◆ Is the pupil making progress?
- ◆ Can the pupil apply understanding, knowledge and skills in a variety of situations?
- ◆ Does the pupil attempt a range of approaches to problems?
- ◆ Does the pupil enjoy the work?
- ◆ Is the pupil actively involved?
- ◆ Does the pupil offer his/her own starting point/extension?
- ◆ Does the pupil communicate mathematics effectively – orally and in writing?
- ◆ Does the pupil sometimes achieve unexpected outcomes?
- ◆ Was the pupil capable of learning any new skills necessary for the completion of the activity?

Mathematical understanding is improved when pupils interact with people and manipulate materials in a wide variety of situations.

When a pupil comes up with something that appears initially to be off the track, hold back from immediately implying that this is the case! How about keeping it as a 'further idea' for later?

Appropriate data

Main focus

Making sense of problems described in words and charts

Content

Applying the four operations to solve problems

Representations of data

Notes for teachers

Discuss one or two problems similar to the pupil task sheets as a class.

Using examples, ensure that all pupils are clear about what they should do.

Ask pupils to do the activity on their own. (*Note:* teachers might decide to pair pupils to help weak readers.)

When most pupils have finished, discuss and compare results. A helpful variation is to ask pupils to discuss and check their work in small groups.

Learning outcomes

The pupils are able to:

- express themselves clearly in both speech and writing, and develop reading skills;
- construct sensible questions;
- choose sensible data;
- eliminate data not needed;
- use symbols to translate and solve problems;
- interpret and criticise mathematical representations.

Evaluation

Could the pupils:

- choose reasonable numbers?
- find correct answers?
- show correct procedures for calculating answers (appropriate to individual pupils' levels)?
- understand standard procedures if used?
- choose and exclude appropriate facts?
- show an understanding of terminology used?
- justify their answers?

Further activity

The class can be involved in choosing the ten best 'complete and solve' problems, which could be set as homework.

Offer pupils calculations such as '£4.53 + £2.29 = £6.82' and ask them to make up appropriate problems to represent the given information.

Ask pupils to collect misleading representations from newspapers, etc., for class discussion.

Resources

Copies of pupil task sheets; additional examples for initial discussion

Complete and solve

UNIT 1 Appropriate data

Here is an incomplete problem:

At the weekend, Tom, George and Jo earned £25.50 washing cars.

What else do you need to add to make it into a problem to solve?

Solve your problem.

For the two following examples, find the answer in each case and write it in the workspace.

Gemma wrote:

At the weekend, Tom, George and Jo earned £25.50 washing cars. They split the money equally. How much did each one receive?

Carol wrote:

At the weekend, Tom, George and Jo earned £25.50 washing cars. Tom kept £12.50 because he bought the cleaning materials. How much did George and Jo take home?

Now complete the following problems and solve them:

1 Mount Everest is 8850 metres high and Ben Nevis is 1340 metres high.

2 A hotel is 42 metres high and each floor is 3.5 metres high.

Complete and solve

3 Three parcels weigh 2.4 kg, 1.8 kg and 723 g.

....

....

....

4 A piece of string is cut into lengths of 1.2 m, 45 cm, 625 mm and 0.35 m.

....

....

....

5 A school wants to take a party of 260 pupils to visit a museum. They decide to go by coach.

....

....

....

6 The minute hand of a clock travels through 30° every 5 minutes. The clock is started at 7.20am.

....

....

....

7 Richard weighs 51.9 kg. He weighs 2.6 kg more than Felicity and 867g less than Simon.

....

....

....

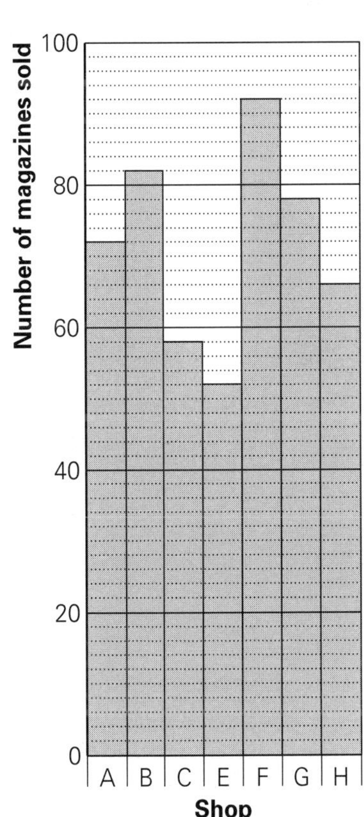

8 The graph shows the result of a survey of sales of a monthly magazine from different shops.

....

....

....

Complete and solve

9 This pie chart shows how Sara spends a 24-hour day.

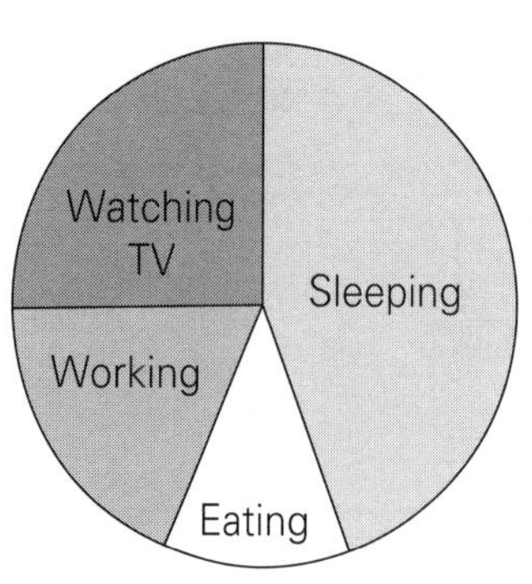

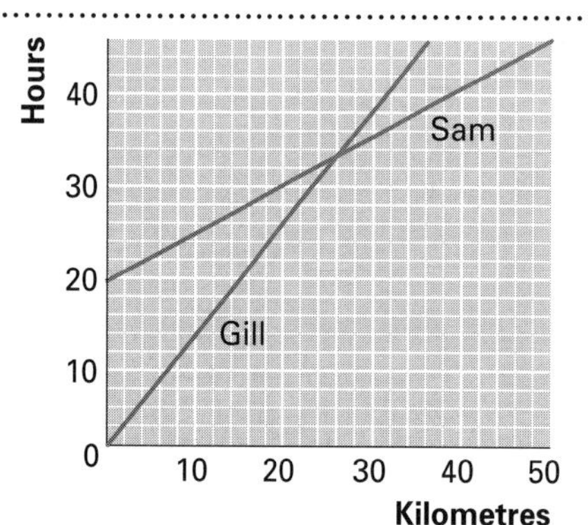

10 This graph shows the journeys made by Sam and Gill.

°F
+50
+40
+30
+20
+10
0
–10
–20
°C
–30
–20
–10
+10
+20

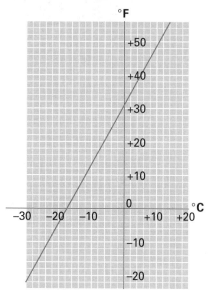

11 This graph can be used to convert temperature from Fahrenheit to centigrade or vice versa.

The right information

Some problems give more facts than you need. Cross out the information that you do not need to solve the problems below. Then solve the problems.

1 A fish tank for six goldfish is 90 cm long, 30 cm wide and 47 cm high. It is to be filled with water to a height of 35 cm. What will be the volume of the water?

....

2 The time in New York is 5 hours behind the time in London and the time in Los Angeles is 8 hours behind London. What will be the time in London when it is 8.00am in New York?

....

3 Anya scored 95 marks in a test. The pass mark is 60%. If the test was marked out of 150, how many marks must a pupil get to pass?

....

4 A disc jockey plays two records. The first one lasts for 3 minutes 25 seconds and the second one for 2 minutes 41 seconds. The cost of the two records was £5.37. Find the total playing time for the two records.

....

5 Sixty people raised £400 in a sponsored walk. Half of them were children and ¼ of them were girls. Each adult raised £4. How much money was raised by the children?

....

....

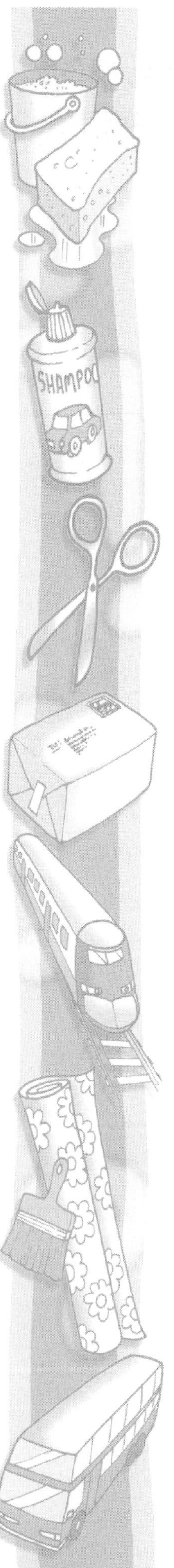

The right information

6 Sunil took two parcels to the post office. They weighed 9.5 kg altogether. The parcels cost £7.28 to send. One parcel weighed 3.37 kg more than the other. What was the weight of each parcel?

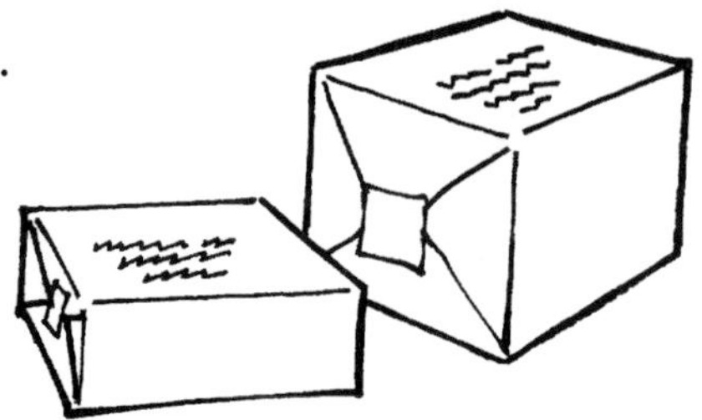

....

7 The train leaves a station at 3.45pm. It makes seven stops and the journey takes 2½ hours. What time does it arrive?

....

8 A 5-litre can of paint covers 12 m^2 of wall. The cost of wallpaper to cover a wall 6 m by 2.5 m would be £13.50. If the paint costs £11.50 for 5 litres, how much would it cost to paint the wall?

....

Sensible charts

Look at Lisa's letter:

1 Why does Lisa think this graph could be misleading?

....

....

....

....

2 What measurements are being represented?

....

....

....

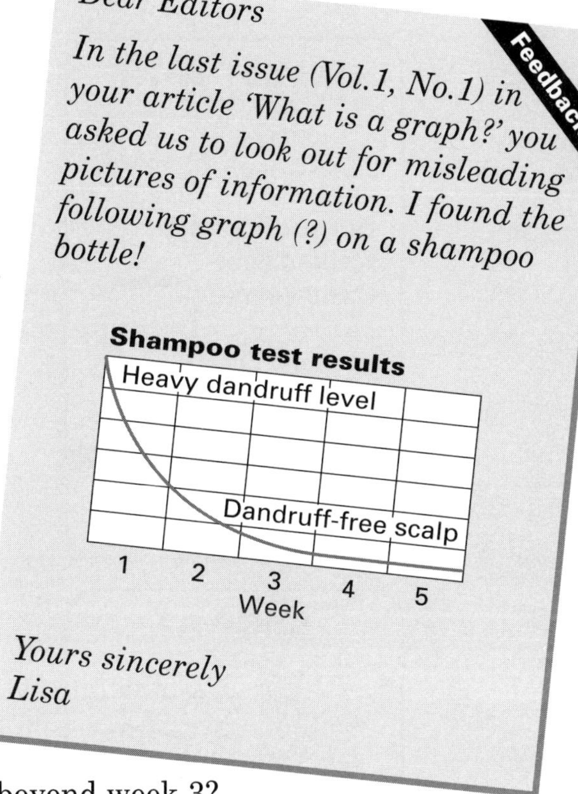
Dear Editors

In the last issue (Vol.1, No.1) in your article 'What is a graph?' you asked us to look out for misleading pictures of information. I found the following graph (?) on a shampoo bottle!

Yours sincerely
Lisa

3 Do you need to use the shampoo beyond week 3?

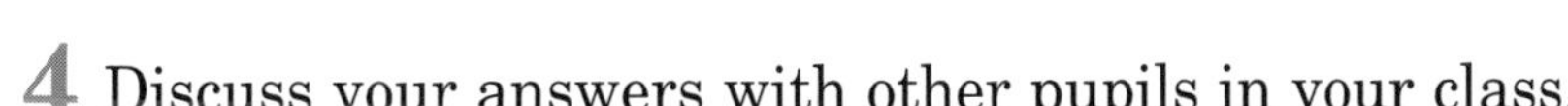

4 Discuss your answers with other pupils in your class.

Now look at this advert. Is this a sensible way to represent information? Give reasons for your answer.

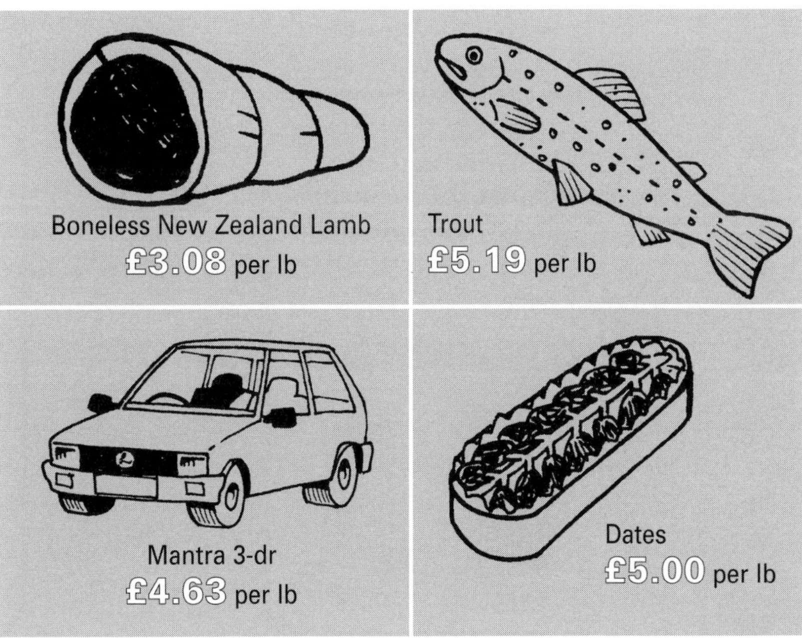

Sensible charts

Look at each of the following charts. For each diagram, write down why you think that it could be misleading.

INVEST WITH
RICHMAN
Our profits have *trebled* over three years
1982
£½ m
1983
£1 m
1984
£1½ m

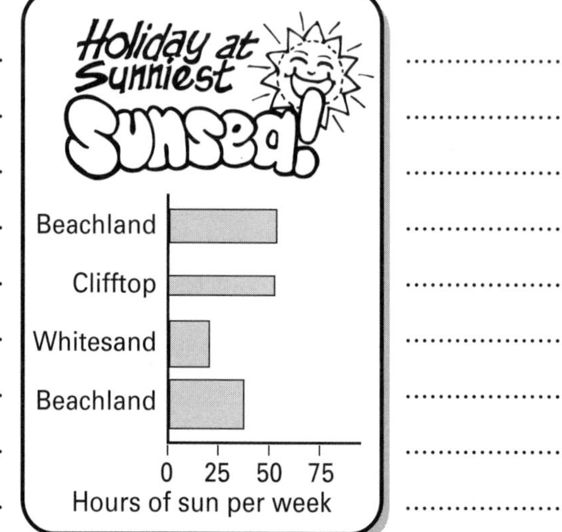

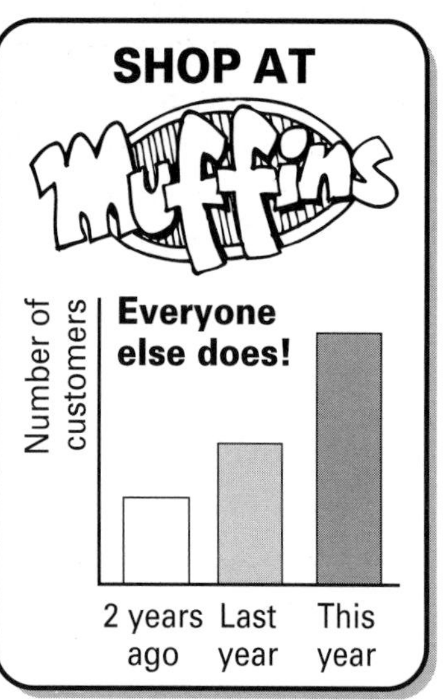

SHOP AT
Muffins
Everyone else does!
Number of customers
2 years ago
Last year
This year

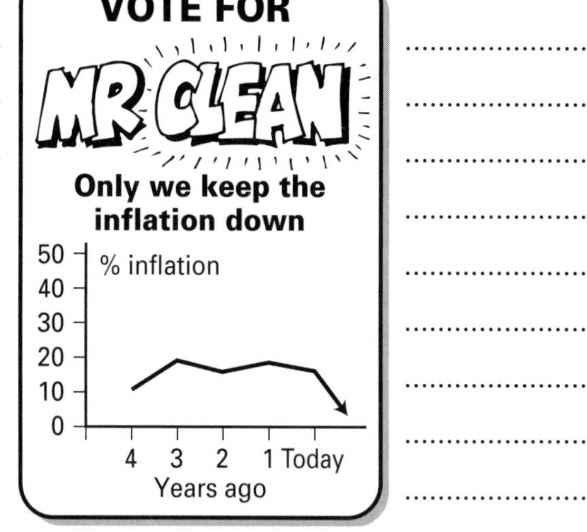

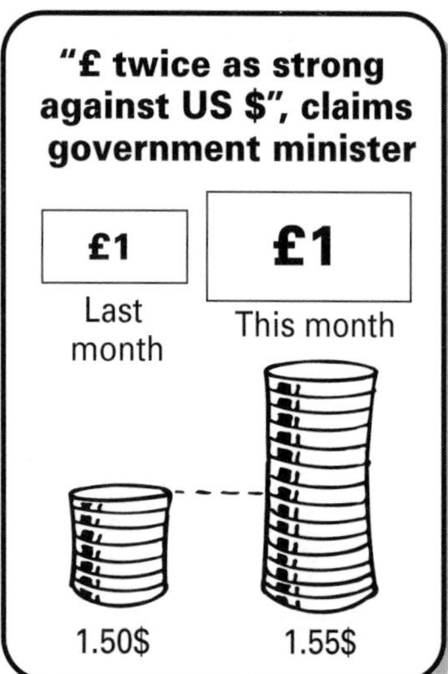

Colour TV

HP available on EASY TERMS

Cash £200

HP at 20% p.a. over 2 years

Place value

Main focus

Using and extending the understanding of place value

Content

Recognising, recording, manipulating and grouping numbers

Practice in addition and subtraction of whole and decimal numbers

Notes for teachers

In order for pupils to perform operations with multi-digit numbers, a strong understanding of place value is needed. It would be helpful to use one example as a whole-class exercise.

Although these activities have been written so that pupils can work individually, they do form productive class and small-group activities. Class and group discussions help to clarify misconceptions and facilitate understanding.

Special attention needs to be given to zero as a place holder.

It is not usual for pupils to encounter very small decimal fractions or very large numbers in everyday contexts. Other subject areas could offer appropriate examples for discussion, for example science, geography.

Learning outcomes

The pupils are able to:

- read, write and order whole and decimal numbers;
- state the place value of any digit in a given number;
- place a set of decimal numbers in ascending or descending order;
- apply their knowledge of odd, even, largest, smallest, etc.

Evaluation

Could the pupils:

- use the concept of place value in whole numbers and decimals?
- match the written numbers with corresponding numerals?
- compare and order the sizes of numbers, including decimals?

Further activity

All activities could be adapted to include larger numbers (additional place value spinners have been included for you to use). Pupils should have a good understanding of numbers up to a million before they undertake activities with numbers greater than this.

Pupils could be asked to provide examples of decimal fractions smaller than tenths for classroom discussion.

Resources

Copies of pupil task sheets; digit and place value spinners (p.27) to be photocopied onto thin card

Digit arrangements

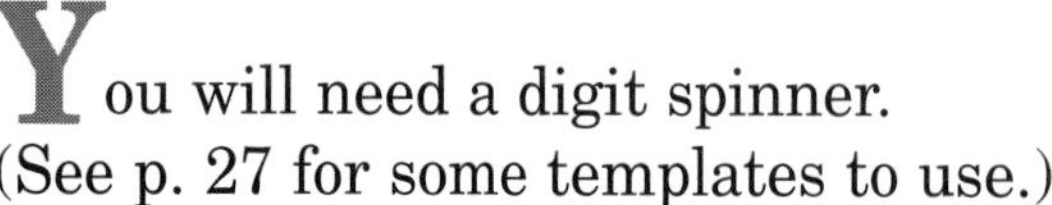

UNIT 2 Place value

You will need a digit spinner. (See p. 27 for some templates to use.)

Spin the digit spinner five times. Write down your digits, in any order, in the boxes at the top of the left-hand column below.

Using all five of your digits once only, make the best numbers you can to fit the statements below. (Some may be impossible!)

Try again with different digits and write your answers in the right-hand column.

	Round 1	Round 2
	☐☐☐☐☐	☐☐☐☐☐
1 Largest possible number		
2 Smallest possible number		
3 Number nearest to 50 000		
4 Largest even number		
5 Smallest odd number		
6 Even number nearest to 60 800		
7 Odd number closest to 35 000		
8 Largest number between 46 320 and 57 040		
9 Smallest number between 72 500 and 82 500		
10 Smallest odd number between 37 000 and 48 000		

Dot to dot

Start at the smallest number and join the dots in order from the lowest to the highest.

Make a list of all the numbers in order.

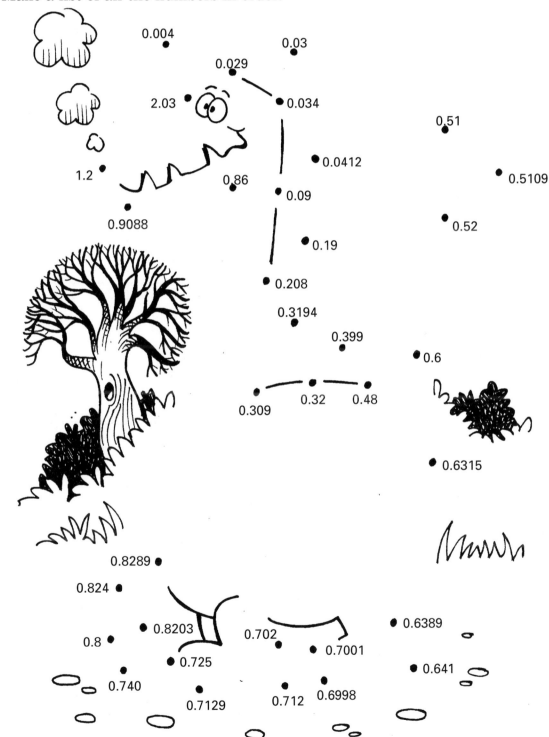

0.004
0.03
0.029
2.03
0.034
0.51
0.0412
1.2
0.86
0.5109
0.09
0.9088
0.52
0.19
0.208
0.3194
0.399
0.6
0.309
0.32
0.48
0.6315
0.8289
0.824
0.6389
0.8203
0.8
0.702
0.7001
0.725
0.641
0.740
0.7129
0.712
0.6998

Find the number

Find the number and put a ring around it in the number grid. Then write it down correctly in the space provided. The following one has been done for you:

7 hundreds,
3 ones,
9 thousands,
5 tens

9753

3	6	8	3	1	9	0	7	5	6
1	6	4	8	9	5	0	4	3	3
3	7	5	8	4	2	5	7	0	0
0	9	7	5	3	7	8	5	3	2
9	7	8	2	3	1	8	7	6	5
6	8	5	0	8	1	1	7	6	9
5	6	7	3	2	9	2	1	0	7
4	4	8	7	2	0	7	1	2	3
5	9	3	5	2	8	1	4	8	6
2	2	3	1	0	8	3	9	4	1

1 6 ones, 20 thousands, 2 hundreds, 7 tens

2 6 thousands, 8 tens, 4 hundreds, 9 ones

3 7 hundreds, 25 thousands

4 7 ones, 1 hundred, 1 ten, 8 thousands, 5 hundred thousands

5 1 thousand, 9 ones, 1 hundred

6 8 thousands, 6 hundreds, 4 tens, 9 ones

7 8 ten thousands, 8 thousands, 4 tens, 5 hundreds, 5 ones

8 3 millions, 1 hundred thousand, 8 thousands, 4 ones, 9 tens, 3 hundreds

9 2 hundreds, 1 ten, 3 ten thousands, 7 thousands, 8 ones

Find the number

10 7 tens, 7 ones, 7 thousands, 5 hundreds

11 7 tens, 3 hundreds, 9 ones

12 5 ones, 9 hundreds, 3 ten thousands, 6 tens

13 71 thousands, 9 tens, 1 hundred

14 19 thousands, 5 ones, 7 tens

15 5 hundreds, 2 tens, 8 thousands

16 6 ones, 8 thousands, 7 hundreds, 3 tens

17 5 hundred thousands, 1 one, 3 hundreds, 9 ten thousands, 7 thousands, 6 tens

18 3 hundreds, 6 tens, 8 ones

19 7 ones, 3 tens, 7 thousands

20 7 ones, 4 millions, 2 hundreds, 4 hundred thousands, 8 ten thousands, 7 thousands

Make 1

Draw a loop around decimal numbers that add up to 1 whole in the horizontal, vertical or diagonal direction. Two examples have been done for you.

0.6	0.4	0.3	0.1	0.6	0.04	0.05	0.7	0.8	0.2
0.2	0.5	0.6	0.7	0.2	0.09	0.5	0.8	0.1	0.4
0.2	0.05	0.72	0.2	0.55	0.07	0.6	0.46	0.72	0.2
0.4	0.34	0.6	0.36	0.3	0.1	0.2	0.22	0.4	0.1
0.1	0.65	0.35	0.15	0.6	0.04	0.2	0.55	0.36	0.05
0.44	0.7	0.15	0.02	0.13	0.66	0.1	0.15	0.28	0.25
0.06	0.54	0.2	0.2	0.76	0.1	0.1	0.3	0.5	0.17
0.1	0.35	0.6	0.05	0.25	0.7	0.8	0.75	0.04	0.6
0.45	0.2	0.1	0.15	0.2	0.2	0.35	0.15	0.15	0.4
0.9	0.85	0.1	0.55	0.3	0.65	0.55	0.2	0.05	0.3

Spot the mistakes

Natalie wrote **$12 + 58 = 17.8$**

How will you re-write this so that the answer *can* be 17.8?

Now re-write the following correctly so that the answers make sense.
Note: do not alter the answer!

1 $9 + 12 - 3 = 7.2$ ....

2 $6 + 25 - 71 = 1.4$ ....

3 $18 - 9 = 0.9$ ....

4 $46 - 9 = 45.1$ ....

5 $731 + 27 = 7.58$ ....

6 $18 + 9 = 2.7$ ....

7 $101 + 25 = 103.5$ ....

8 $512 + 23 - 46 = 282$ ....

9 $312 - 206 + 151 - 9 = 29.75$ ....

10 $452 - 789 + 315 - 642 = 34.04$ ....

Decimal magic squares

Do you remember magic squares like this:

6	7	2
1	5	9
8	3	4

where all the rows, columns and diagonals add up to the same number?

Look at the magic squares below. You have been given the sum for each of the rows, columns and diagonals – but the decimal points have been left out. In each case, put in the decimal point so that the puzzle works.

4	7	14	9
13	10	3	8
10	60	15	12
16	11	20	50

Sum = 3.4

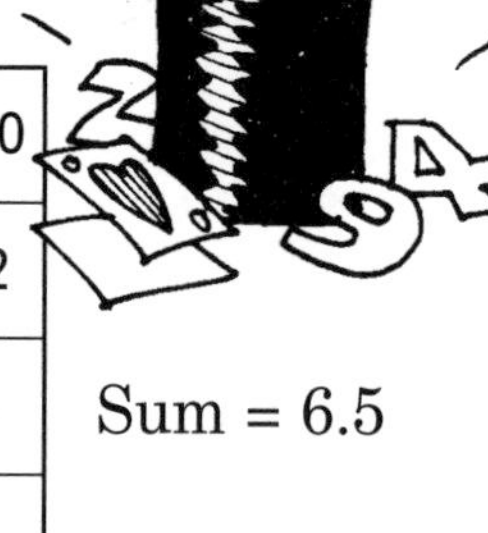

190	20	20	10	230
4	16	90	14	22
180	11	130	15	8
21	120	17	100	5
3	24	60	25	7

Sum = 6.5

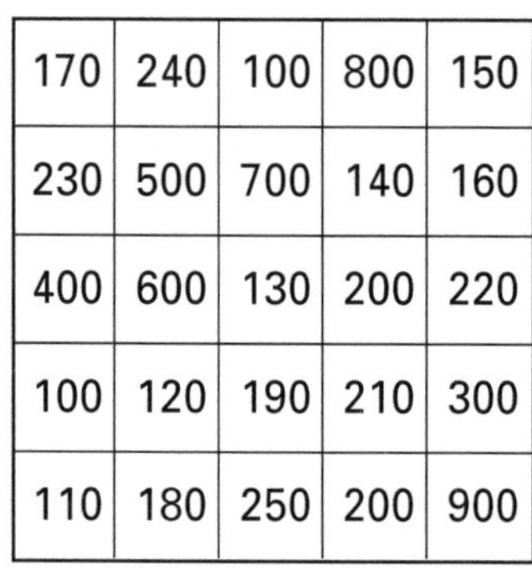

170	240	100	800	150
230	500	700	140	160
400	600	130	200	220
100	120	190	210	300
110	180	250	200	900

Sum = 65

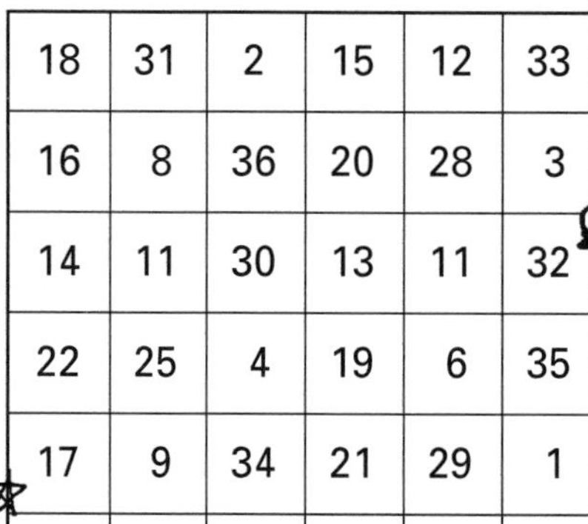

18	31	2	15	12	33
16	8	36	20	28	3
14	11	30	13	11	32
22	25	4	19	6	35
17	9	34	21	29	1
24	27	5	23	25	7

Sum = 11.1

Spin and score

UNIT 2 Place value

A game for two or more players

You will need:

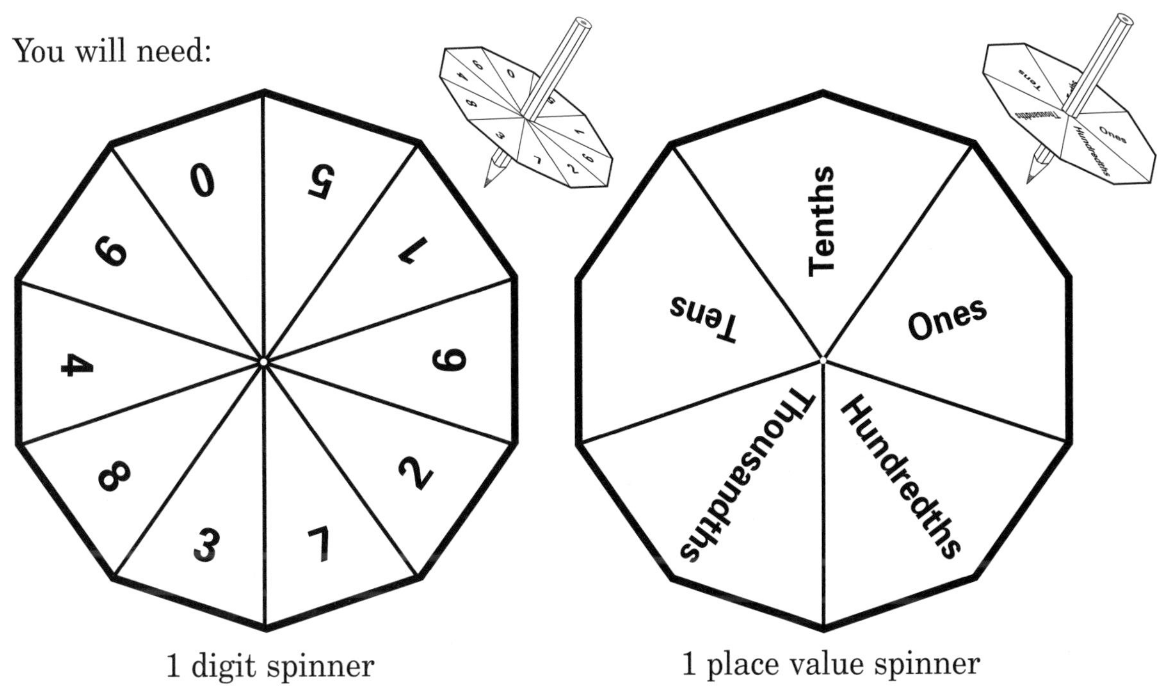

1 digit spinner

1 place value spinner

How to play

1 Each player spins the digit spinner. The player with the highest score starts.

2 Spin both spinners. Write the digit in the correct place on your score card. For example, if you spin a '7' on your digit spinner and a 'tenths' on your place value spinner, you will write the '7' in here:

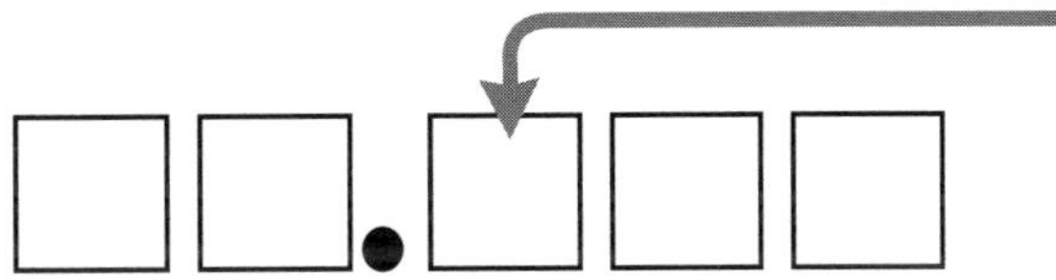

3 The next player has a go.

4 Take it in turns until every space is filled. If your space is already filled with a number, you miss a turn.

5 The player who makes the smallest number wins the round.

Spin and score

Player 1

Round 1			•			
Round 2			•			
Round 3			•			
Round 4			•			
Round 5			•			
Round 6			•			
Round 7			•			
Round 8			•			
Round 9			•			
Round 10			•			

Player 2

Round 1			•			
Round 2			•			
Round 3			•			
Round 4			•			
Round 5			•			
Round 6			•			
Round 7			•			
Round 8			•			
Round 9			•			
Round 10			•			

Place value and digit spinners

0 5 1 9 2 7 3 8 4 6

0 5 1 9 2 7 3 8 4 6

Tenths Ones Hundredths Thousandths Tens

Tenths Ones Hundredths Thousandths Tens

Hundreds Ten-thousands Ones Hundred-thousands Tens Millions Hundred-millions Ten-millions Thousands

Hundreds Ten-thousands Ones Hundred-thousands Tens Millions Hundred-millions Ten-millions Thousands

Mathematical understanding is improved when pupils' own experiences are used appropriately as a source of learning activities.

Encourage pupils to look for connections between old and new situations, ideas and skills, and to ask themselves whether something they did previously might be of use in solving their new problems.

Exact and approximate measures

UNIT 3

Main focus

Sensible measures and their relationships

Content

Measurements – estimates, distance, time and speed

Notes for teachers

Pupils should already be experienced in using a range of everyday objects to compare and order lengths.

The 'Measuring up' task is best carried out in pairs. Pupils should be encouraged to be as accurate as possible within the context. Levels of accuracy could form a useful class discussion.

The emphasis of the 'Flying books' task is on finding approximate equivalents, not on finding an exact answer. It would be helpful to start this activity with a discussion on 'How long would a book take to read?'

Learning outcomes

The pupils are able to:

- estimate and measure objects in their environment;
- select units appropriate to the objects measured;
- see the relationship between distance, time and speed.

Evaluation

Could the pupils:

- make sensible estimates of various sizes?
- measure accurately in centimetres and millimetres?
- compare and talk about relative measures?
- check their work?

Further activity

Books such as *The Guinness Book of Records* and *The Book of Comparisons* (Penguin Books) have a large collection of fascinating number facts. Pupils could be asked to collect data from their own environment, for example the population of their town, and use this to make comparisons with the biggest/smallest town. Similarly, their own measurements of speeds, heights, etc., can be compared with world record measurements.

Make up questions such as 'If 1 million 5p coins were placed on top of each other, how tall would the pile be? If they were placed end to end, how long would the line be?'

Resources

Copies of pupil task sheets; pieces of string; tape measures; rulers

Sensible measurements?

Look at the measurements. Say which ones are sensible and which are not by putting a circle around the correct answer. If you think the measurement is *not* sensible, write down what *would* be sensible, and say why.

One washing load of laundry weighs 15 kg.
Sensible/Not sensible

....

....

....

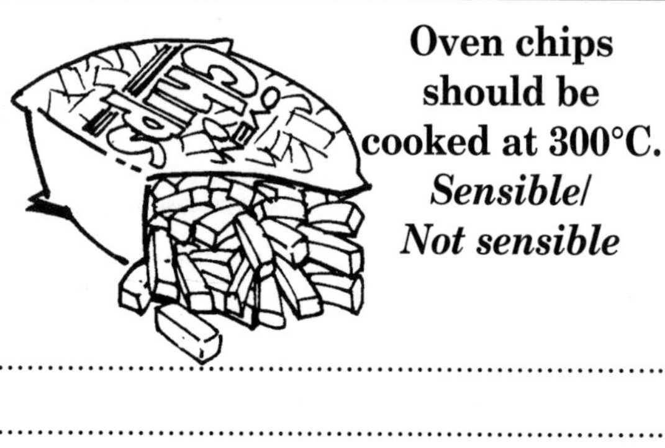

Oven chips should be cooked at 300°C.
Sensible/ Not sensible

....

....

....

The height of a low bridge could be 3 metres.
Sensible/Not sensible

....

....

....

One of the highest recorded temperatures on the earth is 180°C.
Sensible/Not sensible

....

....

....

The width of a heavy goods vehicle is 2 metres.
Sensible/ Not sensible

....

....

....

Sensible measurements?

An electric kettle holds about 13 pints.
Sensible/ Not sensible

....

....

....

The average weight of an adult is 147 kg.
Sensible/Not sensible

....

....

....

....

....

....

A mug of tea holds 642 ml.
Sensible/ Not sensible

....

....

....

....

....

The mass of an adult African elephant is about 6300 kg.
Sensible/Not sensible

....

....

....

....

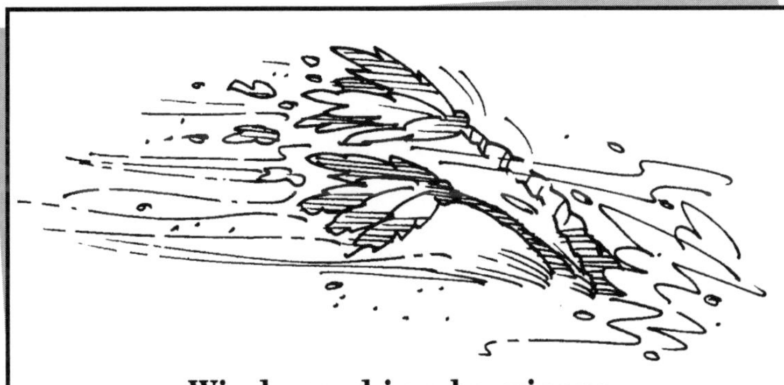

Wind speed in a hurricane could be as much as 125 km/h.
Sensible/Not sensible

....

....

Measuring up

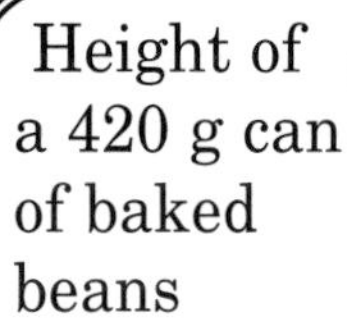

Height of a 420 g can of baked beans

My guess ....

My measurement ....

Height of a 220 g can of baked beans

My guess ....

My measurement ....

Height of a 33 cl can of coke

My guess ....

My measurement ....

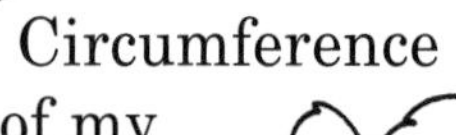

Circumference of my head

My guess ....

My measurement ....

Length of these lines

My guess ....

My measurement ....

Thickness of 50 A4 sheets of paper

My guess ....

My measurement ....

Difference in height between when you hold your breath in and when you breathe out

My guess ....

My measurement ....

Diameter of 2p, 5p and 10p coins

My guesses ....

....

....

My measurements ....

....

....

Height of twenty 2p coins

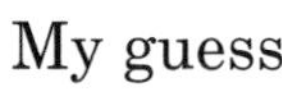

My guess ....

My measurement ....

Diameter of a hose pipe

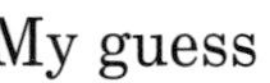

My guess ....

My measurement ....

Circumference of a tennis ball

My guess ....

My measurement ....

Dimensions of a CD case

My guess ....

My measurement ....

Average speeds

Use the 'average speed' nomogram on the next page to help you answer the following questions as accurately as you can.

Example
To find the average speed for a cyclist travelling 90 kilometres in 3 hours, join the 90 on the distance line with the 3 on the time line and find the answer on the middle line.

Now try these:

1 Find the average speed of:

(a) a person walking 26 kilometres in 7½ hours ....

(b) a cyclist travelling 82 km in 3.4 hours ....

(c) an ostrich covering 15 km in 1.2 hours ....

2 Find the time taken for the following journeys:

(a) a car travelling 90 km at an average speed of 55 km an hour ....

(b) a motorcyclist travelling 100 km at 42 km an hour ....

(c) a marathon runner, running for 26 km at 9 km an hour ....

3 How far would the following travel:

(a) a person walking for 2½ hours at an average speed of 5½ km/h? ....

(b) a cyclist travelling for 3½ hours at an average speed of 23 km/h? ....

(c) a bus travelling for 1½ hours at an average speed of 39 km/h? ....

Average speeds

A nomogram for distance, time and average speed

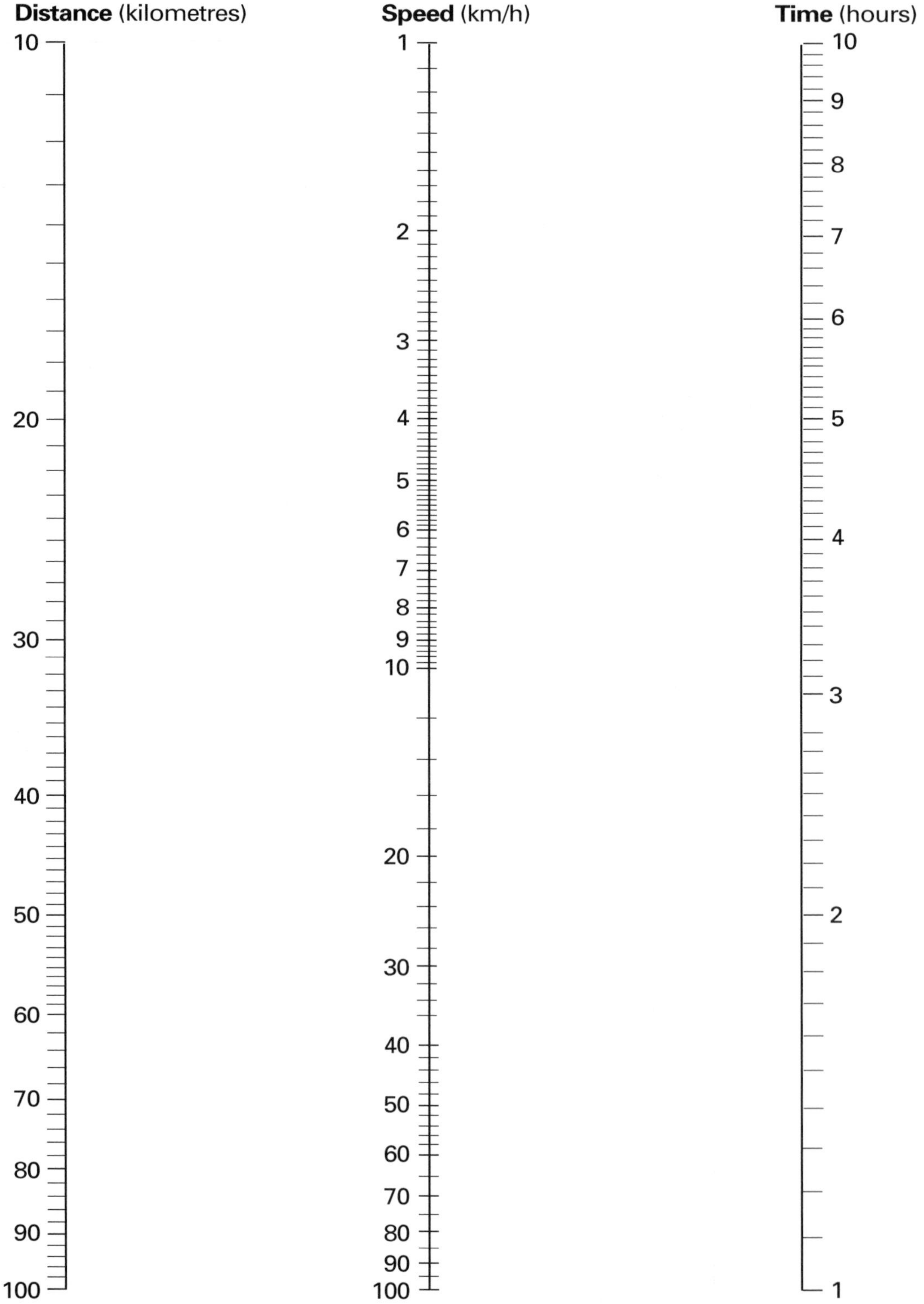

Distance (kilometres): 10, 20, 30, 40, 50, 60, 70, 80, 90, 100

Speed (km/h): 1, 2, 3, 4, 5, 6, 7, 8, 9, 10, 20, 30, 40, 50, 60, 70, 80, 90, 100

Time (hours): 10, 9, 8, 7, 6, 5, 4, 3, 2, 1

Flying books

A bookshop advertised some of its books as follows:

If you plan to enjoy one of the current favourites, how far will it actually take you? Based on average reading speeds, we plotted the air miles contained within some popular titles on sale in our bookshop.

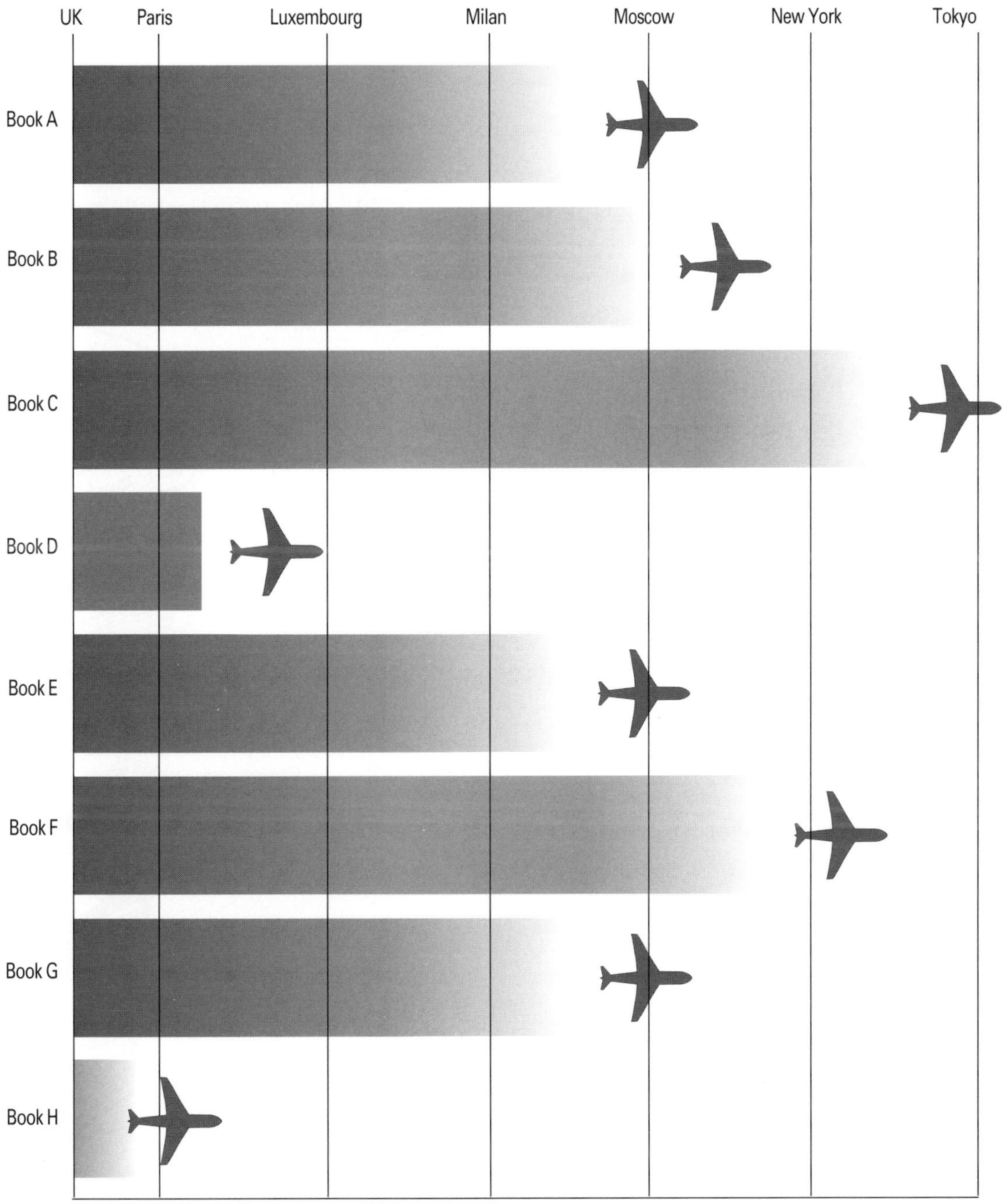

UK | Paris | Luxembourg | Milan | Moscow | New York | Tokyo

Book A

Book B

Book C

Book D

Book E

Book F

Book G

Book H

Flying books

If the average speed of the aircraft is approximately 400 miles per hour for Europe and 550 miles per hour for other flights, find the approximate time taken to read each of the books.

Destination	Miles from the UK
Paris	215
Luxembourg	325
Milan	625
Moscow	1550
New York	3400
Tokyo	5750

Note: distances are in statute miles on great circle routes, rounded for simplicity.

Carry out an experiment, using a book of your own choice, to estimate the time taken to read one page.

Time taken: ....

Using this information, make an estimate of the number of pages in each book.

Book A: ....
Book B: ....
Book C: ....
Book D: ....
Book E: ....
Book F: ....
Book G: ....
Book H: ....

Conversion and calculation

Main focus

Improving strategies for estimation and conversion

Content

Devising techniques appropriate for estimating and checking

Imperial units in daily use and approximate metric equivalents

Currency exchange

Notes for teachers

Some of these activities would need to be carried out over an extended period.

It would be useful to introduce these activities by having a discussion on estimation and which are sensible units to use. Ask pupils to consider how they could improve on the accuracy of their estimates.

After the activity, talk about the best methods and establish a sensible range of answers.

Methods of recording should be discussed.

A calculator will be helpful for some activities.

Learning outcomes

The pupils are able to:

- calculate accurately;
- read tables correctly;
- make sensible estimates in realistic contexts;
- improve the sense of measures;
- round up or down to give appropriate answers;
- organise and record their work systematically.

Evaluation

Could the pupils:

- read tables in the correct order?
- offer reasonable initial estimates?
- plan and organise their experiments?
- choose an appropriate level of accuracy for the activities?
- communicate their findings in writing?

Further activity

Ask pupils to bring conversion charts from newspapers and work on similar tasks. They could be asked to make a presentation of their methods to the rest of the class.

Resources

Metre rules; measuring tapes; weighing scales; string; scissors; calculators; pupil task sheets

Converting measures and temperature

Petrol prices

Have you heard people complaining about how petrol is now priced in litres? Can you think of a simple way of estimating the number of litres in a gallon?

1 gallon = 4.546 litres
and 1 litre = 0.220 gallons

Here is a conversion chart to help you:

Gallons		Litres
0.220	1	4.546
0.442	2	9.092
0.660	3	13.638
0.880	4	18.184
1.100	5	22.730
1.320	6	27.277
1.540	7	31.823
1.760	8	36.369
1.980	9	40.915

1 If you bought 20 litres, how many gallons would that be?

....

2 Using this information, make a conversion chart for buying petrol.

Per litre	Per gallon	Per litre	Per gallon
65.0p	295.5p	68.0p	
1		1	
2		2	
3		3	
4		4	
5		5	
6		6	
7		7	
8		8	
9		9	
66.0p		69.0p	
1		1	
2		2	
3		3	
4		4	
5		5	
6		6	
7		7	
8		8	
9		9	
67.0p		70.0p	318.2p
1		1	
2		2	
3		3	
4		4	
5		5	
6		6	
7		7	
8		8	
9		9	

Petrol price conversion chart

Converting measures and temperature

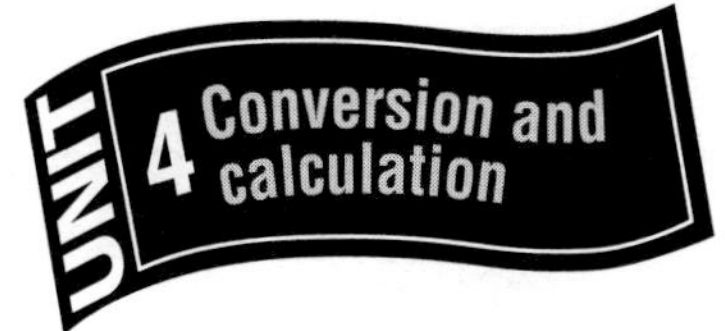

Temperature

A rough rule of thumb for converting centigrade to Fahrenheit is:

Double and add 30

3 Investigate how useful this rule is.

Suggestion

Obtain an instruction book for an electric cooker and check the rule against the conversion chart in it.

4 How well does it work for ice, boiling water, body temperature, a warm day?

....

....

....

5 What would be a rough rule of thumb for converting Fahrenheit to centigrade?

....

....

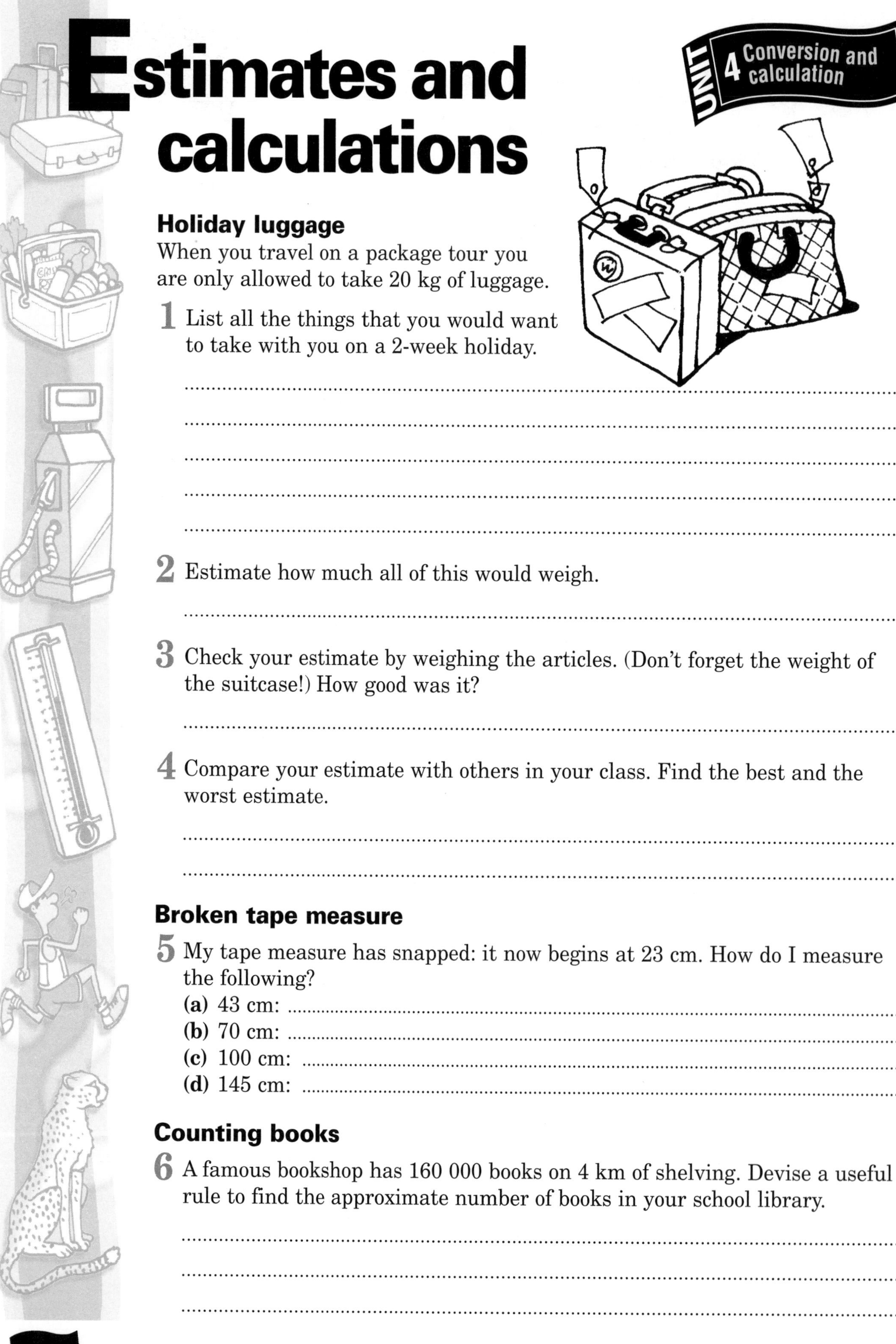

Estimates and calculations

Holiday luggage

When you travel on a package tour you are only allowed to take 20 kg of luggage.

1 List all the things that you would want to take with you on a 2-week holiday.

....

....

....

....

....

2 Estimate how much all of this would weigh.

....

3 Check your estimate by weighing the articles. (Don't forget the weight of the suitcase!) How good was it?

....

4 Compare your estimate with others in your class. Find the best and the worst estimate.

....

....

Broken tape measure

5 My tape measure has snapped: it now begins at 23 cm. How do I measure the following?

(a) 43 cm: ....

(b) 70 cm: ....

(c) 100 cm: ....

(d) 145 cm: ....

Counting books

6 A famous bookshop has 160 000 books on 4 km of shelving. Devise a useful rule to find the approximate number of books in your school library.

....

....

....

What was it like in 1890?

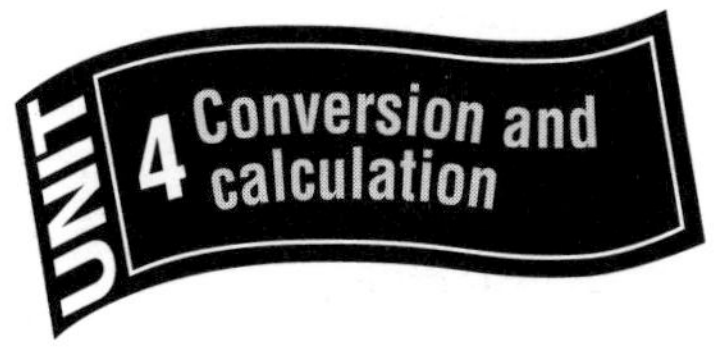

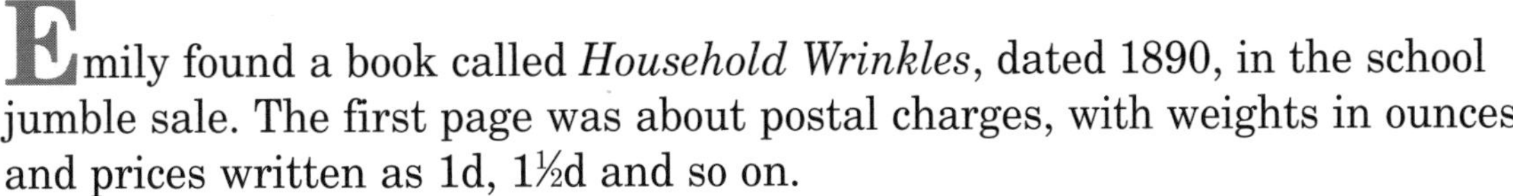

Emily found a book called *Household Wrinkles*, dated 1890, in the school jumble sale. The first page was about postal charges, with weights in ounces and prices written as 1d, 1½d and so on.

Her gran said that this was 'old money' and that life hadn't been the same since decimal money came in, in 1971! 1d stood for 1 penny; there were 12 pennies in a shilling and 20 shillings in 1 pound. Emily already knew that there were 16 ounces in 1 pound weight because the kitchen scales at home were not metric.

The costs of sending letters were shown in a table like this:

Weight	Cost
Under 1 ounce (oz)	1d
1 oz–just under 2 oz	1½ d
2 oz–just under 4 oz	2d
4 oz–just under 6 oz	2½ d
6 oz–just under 8 oz	3d
8 oz–just under 10 oz	3½ d

... and so on

1 What would the cost be of a letter weighing 11 oz?

....

2 What would the cost be of a letter weighing just under 1 lb? (1 pound weight = 16 oz)

....

The book said that 'No letter may exceed 18 inches by 9 inches by 6 inches'. Gran said that this meant you could not send any object longer than 18 inches, but Emily did not agree.

3 What could Emily's rule be? Using this rule, find the longest piece of 6-inch wide card that you can send.

....

....

4 What is the longest piece of Blackpool rock that you could send?

....

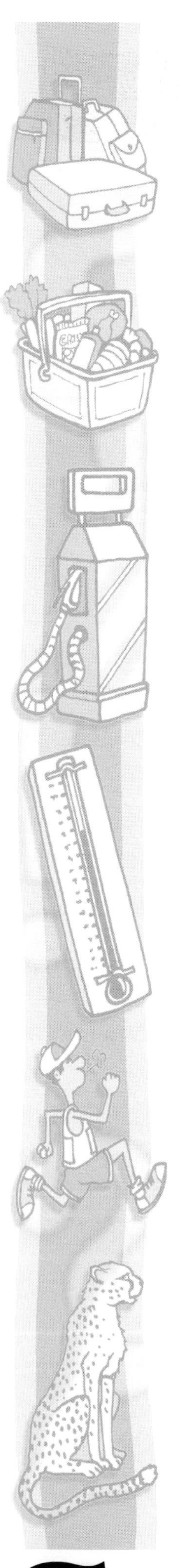

What was it like in 1890?

UNIT 4 Conversion and calculation

The size of the largest parcel that you could send was even stranger: it said that 'No parcel must exceed 3 feet 6 inches in length. Maximum length + girth is 6 feet.' (Girth = width + height)

Emily liked working in centimetres, so translated the measures above to 'No parcel must exceed 105 cm in length. Maximum length + girth is 180 cm.'

5 Suppose we make the length 105 cm. Then maximum width + height = 75 cm. Investigate what dimensions would give you the **maximum volume** for the parcel. You might need to plot a graph, using a calculator or spreadsheet.

6 *Challenge question:* if you could vary the length *up to* 105 cm, would your answer to question 5 change? If so, what is your new maximum volume?

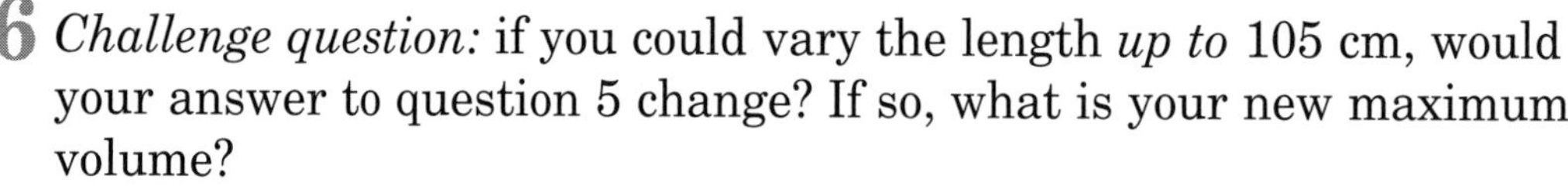

Postal charges in 2002

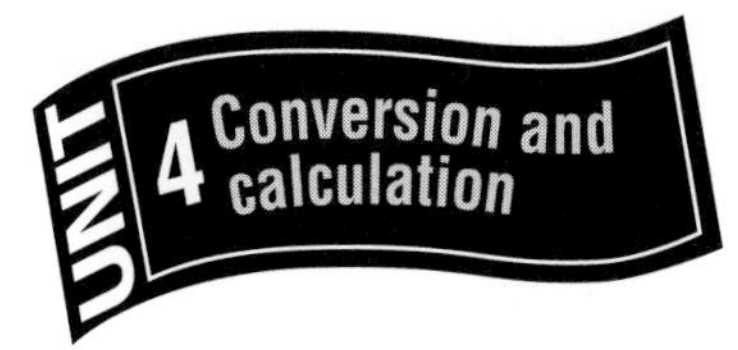

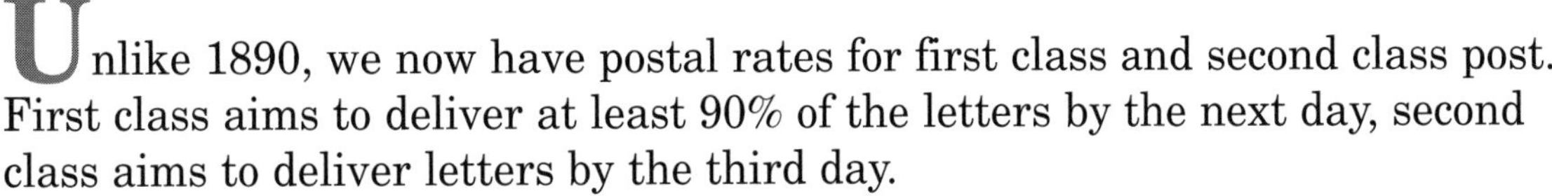

Unlike 1890, we now have postal rates for first class and second class post. First class aims to deliver at least 90% of the letters by the next day, second class aims to deliver letters by the third day.

The table of postal charges includes the following information:

Weight up to	First class	Second class		
60 g	27p	19p		
100 g	41p	33p		
150 g	57p	44p		
200 g	72p	54p		
250 g	84p	66p		
300 g	96p	76p		
350 g	£1.09	87p		
400 g	£1.24	£1.00		
450 g	£1.41	£1.14		
500 g	£1.58	£1.30		
600 g	£1.90	£1.52		
700 g	£2.39	£1.74		

These weights are given in grammes, not in ounces. Of course, first class is more expensive because it is faster.

How does the Post Office decide on what difference there should be between the two charges? Is it a fixed percentage?

To find the percentage increase from second to first: find the increase in pence, then divide this by the second class charge, then multiply by 100.

So for 60 g we calculate (8 ÷ 19) x 100 = 42.1% increase.

1 Fill in the two blank columns in the table above. Call the first one 'Difference in price' and the second 'Percentage increase' and fill in the figures that you calculate. Can you come to any conclusions?

....

....

Postal charges in 2002

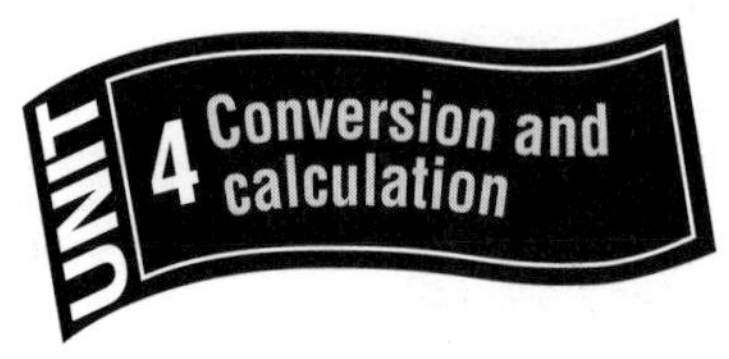

2 The values of postage stamps issued at the present time are as follows: 1p, 2p, 4p, 5p, 8p, 10p, 20p, 33p, 40p, 41p, 45p, 50p, 65p, £1, £1.50, £2, £3, £5

Work out the least number of stamps needed for each of the postal rates in the table on the previous sheet for first and second class postage.

....

....

....

....

....

....

3 How can we compare postal rates for 1890 (see 'What was it like in 1890?' task sheet) and 2002?

Useful facts

1 oz = 28.34 g
1 lb = 0.4536 kg
240d = 100p
1d = 0.42p
1s = 5p

From the table on the 1890 task sheet, we can see that a letter weighing 6 oz cost 3d.

(a) Convert:

6 oz = (6 x 28.34) g = ... g

3d = (3 x 0.42)p = ... p

(b) Use the 2002 table to find the cost of first class postage for a letter of this weight. How many times more expensive is it now?

....

(c) What about second class? How many times more expensive is this?

....

....

....

....

Is it really more expensive in 2002 than in 1890?

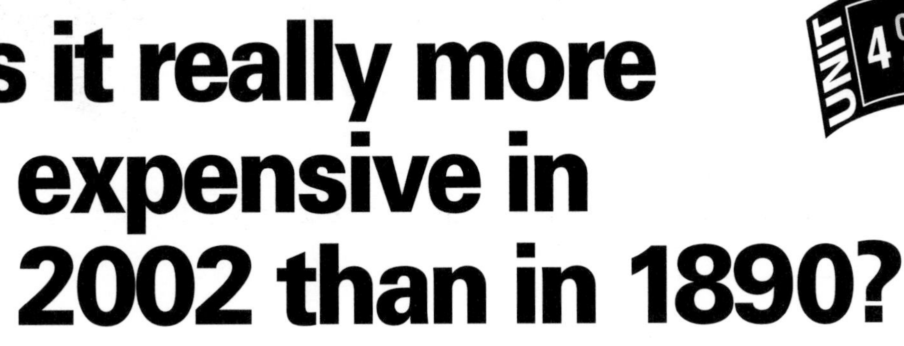

UNIT 4 Conversion and calculation

According to the Bank of England Retail Price Index, the pound could buy 35.87 times as much in 1900 as it could in 1993. This figure is quite close to the answer for second class post (question 3[c] on the 'Postal charges in 1999' task sheet).

How do they work this out?

They could look at wages or cost of houses for the two years in question, but these vary in different parts of the country and the number of home owners is much greater now.

The standard way is to look at the cost of a 'food basket' of essential goods. Of course, fashions in eating change – no hedgehog crisps in 1890!

Here are two 'food baskets', for 1905 and 1993, with adjustments to make them both decimal currency per pound weight.

Food basket (selection)

1905 (per lb unless otherwise stated)	1905 cost	1905 decimal currency per lb	1993 cost (per lb unless otherwise stated)	1993 decimal currency per lb
Butter	1s 2d	5.84p	74p (250 kg)	134.5p
Sugar	0s 3d	1.26p	68p (1 kg)	30.84p
Flour	1s 5d	7.00p	63p (1.5 kg)	20.56p
Tea	1s 6d	7.00p	65p (125 g)	236.40p
Potatoes (20 lb)	0s 10d	0.21p	11p	11p
Cheese	0s 6d	2.50p	176p	176p
Bacon	0s 9d	3.80p	208p	208p
Onions	0s $1\frac{1}{2}$ d	0.63p	22p	22p
Eggs	1s 0d	5.00p	124p	124p
Lard	0s 7d	2.90p	18p	18p
Apples	0s 3d	1.26p	41p	41p
Milk (12 pints)	0s 3d	0.105p per pint	33p per pint	33p
Total	1905:		1993:	

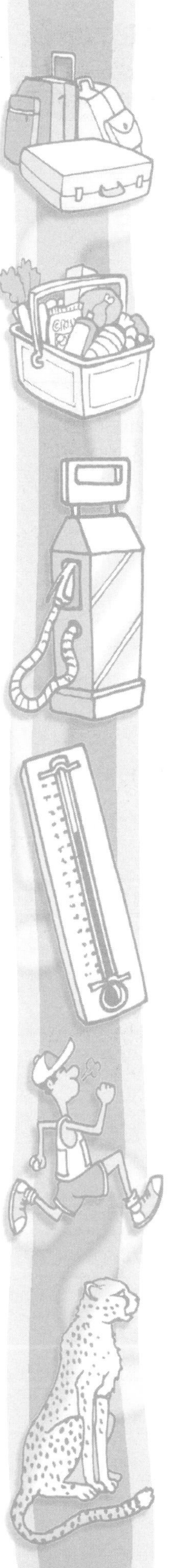

Is it really more expensive in 2002 than in 1890?

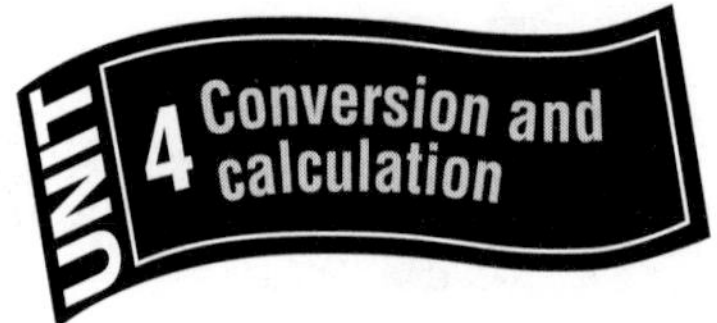

1 Add up the total for 1905 (column 3 figures).

....

2 Add up the total for 1993 (column 5 figures).

....

3 How many times bigger is the second total?

....

4 The Bank of England Retail Price Index suggests that prices are 34.75 times higher in 1993 than in 1905. Does your answer to question 3 suggest to you that food is cheaper now or more expensive? Discuss this with your teacher.

World athletics records

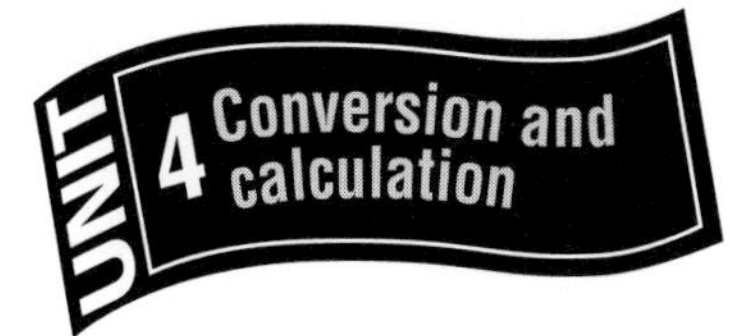

The current records include the following:

Distance	Time	Athlete	Country
100 metres	9.84 seconds	Donovan Bailey	Canada
200 metres	19.32 seconds	Michael Johnson	USA
400 metres	43.29 seconds	'Butch' Reynolds	USA

Donovan Bailey was described as 'the fastest man on earth'.

1 Do the times above agree with this? Can you explain your answer?

....

....

The fastest creatures in nature are:

Mammal:	Cheetah Horse	105 km/h 69 km/h
Bird:	Spine-tailed swift	171 km/h
Fish:	Sailfish	110 km/h

Where does the fastest human fit into this table? The time for the athletes is given in seconds. We can work out the speed in metres per second (m/s) and then convert to kilometres per hour (km/h).

> For example, running **200 metres in 30 seconds** = (200 ÷ 30) m/s.
>
> In 1 hour there are 60 minutes, each containing 60 seconds, so we multiply (200 ÷ 30) × 60 × 60 to give us metres per hour. There are 1000 metres in 1 km, so we divide metres per hour by 1000.

Use your calculator to work out (200 ÷ 30) × 60 × 60 ÷ 1000 = 24 km/h.

2 The calculation for **Michael Johnson** is (200 ÷ 19.32) × 60 × 60 ÷ 1000. Work this out and add it to the bottom row of the table above.

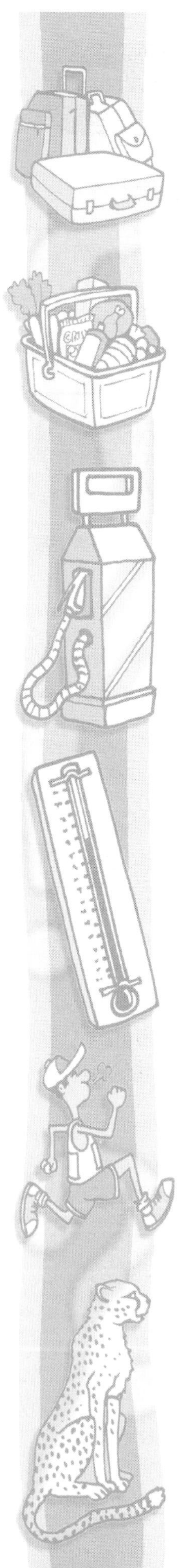

World athletics records

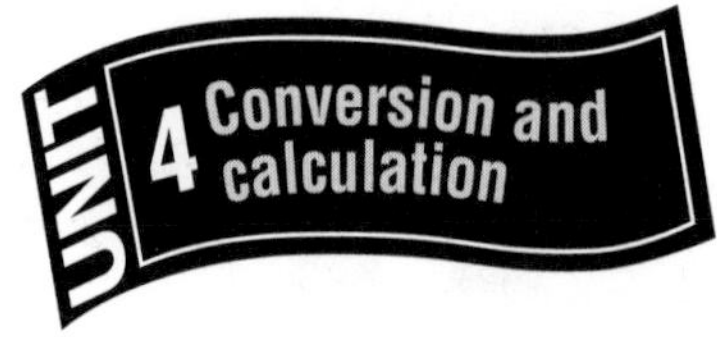

3 Draw a bar graph to show the information in the table, using a vertical scale of 1 cm representing 20 km/h.

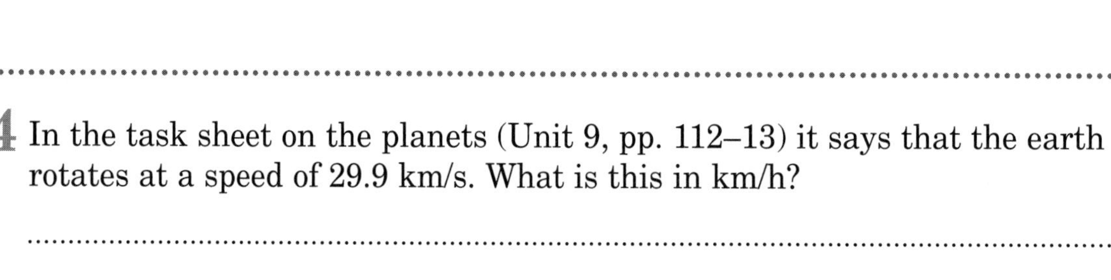

4 In the task sheet on the planets (Unit 9, pp. 112–13) it says that the earth rotates at a speed of 29.9 km/s. What is this in km/h?

....

....

The fastest rail journeys in the world

In the book *Top 10 of Everything, 1998*, the fastest four rail journeys are listed as follows:

Order	Country	Route	Train	Distance (km)	Speed (km/h)	Time (minutes)
1	France	Paris–Lille	TVG	204.2	250.0	
2	Japan	Hiroshima–Kokuni	31 Nozoni	192.0	230.4	
3	Spain	Madrid–Ciudad Real	AVE	170.7	217.9	
4	Germany	Fulda–Kassel	ICE	90.0	200.0	

The **fifth fastest** is the United Kingdom. This is an InterCity 225 train travelling from Stevenage to Doncaster, a distance of 129.13 miles, at an average speed of 110.69 m.p.h.

1 Given the fact that 5 miles is the same distance as 8 km, convert the miles to km and the m.p.h. to km/h and write your answers in the table below.

5	UK	Stevenage–Doncaster	InterCity 225			

To work out the **time** for each journey we have to divide the **distance** by the **speed**. This gives the number of hours; multiply by 60 to find the number of minutes.

For example, for number 1 the time in hours is 204.2 ÷ 250.0 = 0.8168 hours. Multiply this by 60 = 49.0 minutes.

2 Enter this time on the table, then complete the time column for the other four trains. You could use either a calculator or a spreadsheet for this.

Mathematical understanding is improved when pupils are made aware of the relevance of mathematics to their lives.

Help pupils to appreciate the importance of asking questions like, 'Is this sensible?' 'Can I check this for myself?'

Number cards (3 sets)

Note: these cards have been adapted from *Do Discuss Mathscards* (Blackie Chambers, 1972).

Main focus

Decimals (including measures) and mental calculations

Content

Practice with calculations and metric measurements

Notes for teachers

These cards can be used for three purposes:

- Class use – the cards are arranged to go around in a full circle. A pupil starts by reading aloud his/her main number, followed by the question below. This is answered by the pupil who has the answer at the top of the card. This process is repeated until all the cards have been used. The cards can be re-shuffled and the process repeated. An element of urgency can be introduced by timing the activity. Teachers will need to be sensitive to individual pupils' difficulties and read the question/answer if necessary.
- Group use – teachers may wish to divide pupils into groups according to pace. Working together can help them overcome reading and counting difficulties. Pencil and paper can be allowed to deal with more difficult cards.
- Individual use – once pupils have an idea of how the cards work, they can use sets of cards individually. A written record could be kept.

Learning outcomes

The pupils are able to:

- read and interpret mathematical questions fluently;
- understand and work out answers mentally;
- check mental calculations.

Evaluation

Could the pupils:

- read the cards correctly?
- carry out correct calculations?
- establish equivalence between fractions and decimals in the context of mass and length?
- verify calculations using pen-and-paper methods?

Further activity

This idea can be adapted for other mathematical topics or more difficult questions using blank playing cards. (*Note:* see Loop Cards devised by Adrian Pinel, University College, Chichester.)

Resources

Sets of number cards (best photocopied onto thin card)

Decimal cards

1.2 **Subtract 0.72**	**2.26** **Multiply by 10**	**6.3** **Add 1.4**
5.2 **Divide by 0.26**	**0.8** **Add 1.95**	**0.96** **Divide by 0.8**
5.76 **Subtract 3.5**	**7** **Multiply by 0.9**	**0.3** **Add 4.9**
2.5 **Subtract 1.7**	**0.46** **Add 0.5**	**5.4** **Add 0.36**
5.6 **Divide by 0.8**	**21** **Divide by 70**	**25** **Divide by 10**

Decimal cards

46 **Divide by 100**	**0.6** **Multiply by 9**	**1.4** **Multiply by 4**
3.55 **Add 1.7**	**0.25** **Multiply by 100**	**23** **Divide by 0.5**
4.2 **Divide by 7**	**0.2** **Multiply by 7**	**4.3** **Subtract 0.75**
0.48 **Subtract 0.23**	**22.6** **Add 0.4**	**7.7** **Subtract 3.5**
20 **Divide by 100**	**2.75** **Add 1.55**	**5.25** **Multiply by 4**

Mixed calculation cards

88 **Divide by 8, then add 4**	**66** **Subtract 6**	**110** **Divide by 10, then add 133**
57 **Add 51**	**44** **Divide by 4, then add 61**	**43** **Add 41**
11 **Multiply by 6**	**61** **Add 49**	**132** **Divide by 11, then add 45**
72 **Divide by 6, then add 87**	**48** **Divide by 4, then add 31**	**36** **Divide by 3, then add 43**
108 **Divide by 9, then add 49**	**33** **Divide by 3, then add 85**	**19** **Add 17**

Mixed calculation cards

23 **Add 25**	**55** **Divide by 5, then add 28**	**39** **Add 38**
15 **Add 18**	**120** **Divide by 10, then add 7**	**22** **Divide by 2, then add 12**
12 **Add 120, then divide by 12**	**77** **Divide by 7, then add 13**	**24** **Divide by 2, then add 76**
99 **Divide by 9, then add 54**	**60** **Divide by 5, then add 10**	**144** **Divide by 12**
96 **Divide by 8, then add 120**	**84** **Divide by 7, then add 32**	**65** **Add 55**

Metric measure cards

0.9 How many millilitres are there in 3 litres?	**250 g** Add 60 g, 40 g and 25 g	**150 mm** 2.5 cm. How many mm is this?
40 km Two towns are 35 km apart. How far is it from one to the other and back again?	**8** How many millimetres are there in 1 centimetre?	**2.2 cm** 9 mm. What fraction of a cm is this?
500 g Tea sells in ¼ kg packets. How many grams is this?	**30 mm** 15 cm. How many mm is this?	**200 m** Two towns are 20 km apart. How far is it from one town to the other and back again?
6 litres How many cups holding 250 ml can be filled from a 2-litre teapot?	**100 g** 22 mm. How many cm is this?	**2000 m** Butter sells in ½ kg packets. How many grams is this?
1000 cm or 10 m 3 cm. How many mm is this?	**125 m** How many metres are there in ⅕ kilometre?	**120p** How much milk is in 12 bottles, each holding ½ litre?

Metric measure cards

900 g 1 kg of sweets is divided equally into ten packets. What weight is each packet?	**18 cm** How many metres are there in 2 kilometres?	**500 cm or 5 m** A desk is 50 cm wide. How wide are 20 desks?
1000 m How many metres are there in ⅛ kilometre?	**3000 ml** Pencils cost 10 pence each. What is the total cost of 12 pencils?	**650 ml** Take 100 g away from 1 kg
4 cm Twelve books are each 1.5 cm thick. What is their total thickness?	**100 cm or 1 m** A desk is 50 cm wide. How wide are ten desks?	**100 cm** How many metres are there in 1 kilometre?
125 g Take 350 ml from 1 litre	**25 mm** 40 mm. How many cm is this?	**70 km** A desk is 50 cm wide. How wide are two desks?
10 mm How many centimetres are there in 1 metre?		

Mathematical understanding is improved when pupils are encouraged to use spoken and written language appropriate to their development, in order to gain meaning from their mathematical experiences.

Put up examples of pupils' own questions on display. Invite groups to look at and perhaps work on other groups' suggestions.

Factors, products and primes

Main focus

Reinforcing relationships between two or more numbers, especially factors, multiples and primes

Content

Factors, multiples, primes, sum of primes

Notes for teachers

These tasks assume pupils' familiarity with prime numbers up to 100 and methods such as the Sieve of Eratosthenes.

As an initial introduction to multiples and patterns of number, it might be worth starting by using the 'Patterns in number' triangle grid (p. 71) to investigate patterns for odd numbers, even numbers, multiples of 3, 5 and 10, prime numbers, and multiples of prime numbers.

Encouraging pupils to explain their answers and rules to each other will help them to crystallise definitions and relationships.

Learning outcomes

The pupils are able to:

- ◆ understand the following terms: factor, multiple, divisible, even, odd, square and prime;
- ◆ use the above terms in spotting and in writing down number relationships;
- ◆ extend mental and written computation;
- ◆ use spreadsheets appropriately.

Evaluation

Could the pupils:

- ◆ compute the sum and products correctly?
- ◆ correctly interpret the mathematical terms and symbols used?
- ◆ recall number bonds fluently?
- ◆ express rules in words?

Further activity

Ask pupils to write $n^2 - n + 11$ and investigate the values of n that will give prime numbers. Replace 11 in the expression with other numbers such as 13, 17, 41 to find some good generators of primes.

The product and sum table (p. 60) could be used to explore prime factors.

Resources

Copies of pupil task sheets; dice; cm^2 grid paper; 1–100 number grid (optional); triangle grid; access to the Internet if possible

Spot the numbers

Roll two dice 20 times and record your scores on the chart, using the following rules:

- for the first die you need to square the score and subtract 1 ($n^2 - 1$);
- for the second die you need to double the score and subtract 1 ($2n - 1$).

Multiply your scores together to get the **product**.

Add the scores together to find the **sum**.

Score die 1 ($n^2 - 1$)	Score die 2 ($2n - 1$)	Product ($n^2 - 1$) ($2n - 1$)	Sum ($n^2 - 1$) + ($2n - 1$)

Spot the numbers

From your results, write in all the scores that can fit these statements. (Some may be impossible!)

Chart 1

The product has at least two factors greater than 5.	
The product is a multiple of 3.	
The product is divisible by 6.	
The product is an odd number between 160 and 265.	
The product is divisible by 11.	
The product is a multiple of 5.	
The product has at least four factors.	

Chart 2

The sum is a multiple of 11.	
The sum is divisible by 3 and greater than 20.	
The sum is a multiple of 4 between 30 and 50.	
The sum is a multiple of 2 and 3.	
The sum is a prime number.	
The sum has at least one prime factor.	
The sum is either one bigger or one smaller than a square number.	

Look at your charts. Were there any that were impossible?

What scores would you need to complete the table?

Further challenges

Find the product that has the greatest number of factors.
Find the sum that is an even number and also the sum of two prime numbers.

Prime numbers 1

Is there a pattern for prime numbers? If you look at a number grid arranged in the usual way, i.e. in 10s, then there doesn't seem to be much of a pattern. You may have come across a method called the Sieve of Eratosthenes for doing this. Part of a grid is shown below.

1	**2**	**3**	4	**5**	6	**7**	8	9	10
11	12	**13**	14	15	16	**17**	18	**19**	20
21	22	**23**	24	25	26	27	28	**29**	30
31	32	33	34	35	36	**37**	38	39	40
41	42	**43**	44	45	46	**47**	48	49	50

1 Explain why there are no prime numbers in the 4, 6, 8 and 10 columns.

....

2 Can you predict how many prime numbers there will be in each row of this table? You could extend it to 100 say.

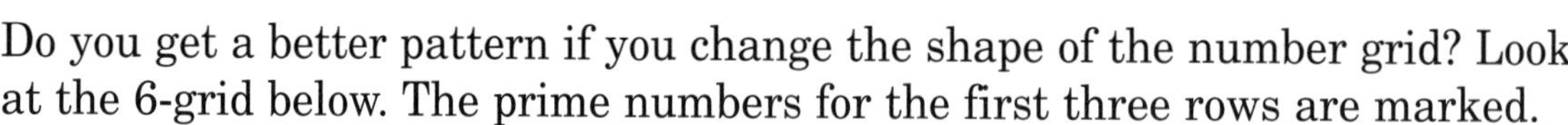

Do you get a better pattern if you change the shape of the number grid? Look at the 6-grid below. The prime numbers for the first three rows are marked.

1	**2**	**3**	4	**5**	6
7	8	9	10	**11**	12
13	14	15	16	**17**	18
19	20	21	22	23	24
25	26	27	28	29	30
31	32	33	34	35	36
37	38	39	40	41	42
43	44	45	46	47	48
49	50	51	52	53	54
55	56	57	58	59	60

Prime numbers 1

3 Complete marking in the prime numbers on the table.

4 Describe any pattern that you can see. Can you predict where on the table the prime numbers will occur?

....

....

5 Extend the 6-grid to say 120, to see if your prediction holds true. (Of course this does not *prove* that it will always be true.)

6 Since we are using a 6-grid, can you explain the pattern in terms of multiples of 6? You might want to add a statement to explain why some numbers do not fit into your pattern.

....

....

In the past, mathematicians have tried to find a formula for prime numbers and have put forward suggestions. One such suggestion was $n^2 - n + 41$ where n is replaced with 1, 2, 3, 4, etc.

For example, for $n = 1$ we get $1 - 1 + 41 = 41$, which is prime; for $n = 2$ we get $4 - 2 + 41 = 43$ (prime); for $n = 3$ we get $9 - 3 + 41 = 47$ (prime).

7 Can you give the *obvious* value of n that does not produce a prime number?

....

8 Use a spreadsheet or calculator to try all the values of n up to your answer to question 7. Write them down. Are they all prime numbers?
If you haven't got an answer to 7, try all values of n up to say 50.

Prime numbers 1

6-grid

1	2	3	4	5	6

6-grid

1	2	3	4	5	6

Prime numbers 2
Using a spreadsheet

You need to have covered the 'Prime numbers 1' task sheet (on pp. 62–3) before attempting this exercise.

You will have found that, after the first row of the 6-grid, all prime numbers came in column 1 or column 5. These numbers could be expressed as one more (or five less) than a multiple of 6, or one less (or five more) than a multiple of 6. There are some numbers in these two columns that are *not* primes, for example 49, which is a square number – factors 7 × 7 – but we do know that if the number does not come in column 1 or 5 of the 6-grid it cannot be prime (except for numbers 2 and 3).

As a first test of the numbers that you found for question 8 on the previous task sheet, find the remainder when the number is divided by 6. If it is 1 or 5 then at least the number is in one of the correct columns.

To use Excel

- In the first column, enter 1 in cell A1. In cell A2, enter =A1 + 1. Drag the bottom right-hand corner down to row 50. You should now have numbers 1 to 50 in the first column.
- In cell B1, enter =A1*A1 – A1 + 41 and press RETURN (ENTER). Drag the bottom right-hand corner of that cell down to row 50. The bottom number should now be 2491.
- For the third column in your spreadsheet, enter =mod(B1,6) into cell C1, where **mod** is the remainder when the formula in B1 is divided by 6. Drag the bottom right corner of that cell down to row 50.
- Look at the numbers in this third column. Did you find that they were all 1 or 5? This means that they are in the correct columns for prime numbers, although remember that there were some numbers in these columns that were not prime (e.g. 49 is square).

Shaun used the school Internet link to search for 'prime numbers'. He found a site that listed the *first 1000 primes*, so he downloaded this to check the numbers in column 2 of his spreadsheet. The list up to 2153 is shown on the next sheet. Use it to check your own.

Prime numbers 2
Using a spreadsheet

Table of primes from the Internet

2	3	5	7	11	13	17	19	23	29
31	37	41	43	47	53	59	61	67	71
73	79	83	89	97	101	103	107	109	113
127	131	137	139	149	151	157	163	167	173
179	181	191	193	197	199	211	223	227	229
233	239	241	251	257	263	269	271	277	281
283	293	307	311	313	317	331	337	347	349
353	359	367	373	379	383	389	397	401	409
419	421	431	433	439	443	449	457	461	463
467	479	487	491	499	503	509	521	523	541
547	557	563	569	571	577	587	593	599	601
607	613	617	619	631	641	643	647	653	659
661	673	677	683	691	701	709	719	727	733
739	743	751	757	761	769	773	787	797	809
811	821	823	827	829	839	853	857	859	863
877	881	883	887	907	911	919	929	937	941
947	953	967	971	977	983	991	997	1009	1013
1019	1021	1031	1033	1039	1049	1051	1061	1063	1069
1087	1091	1093	1097	1103	1109	1117	1123	1129	1151
1153	1163	1171	1181	1187	1193	1201	1213	1217	1223
1229	1231	1237	1249	1259	1277	1279	1283	1289	1291
1297	1301	1303	1307	1319	1321	1327	1361	1367	1373
1381	1399	1409	1423	1427	1429	1433	1439	1447	1451
1453	1459	1471	1481	1483	1487	1489	1493	1499	1511
1523	1531	1543	1549	1553	1559	1567	1571	1579	1583
1597	1601	1607	1609	1613	1619	1621	1627	1637	1657
1663	1667	1669	1693	1697	1699	1709	1721	1723	1733
1741	1747	1753	1759	1777	1783	1787	1789	1801	1811
1823	1831	1847	1861	1867	1871	1873	1877	1879	1889
1901	1907	1913	1931	1933	1949	1951	1973	1979	1987
1993	1997	1999	2003	2011	2017	2027	2029	2039	2053
2063	2069	2081	2083	2087	2089	2099	2111	2113	2129
2131	2137	2141	2143	2153					

Put a ring round the prime numbers that the *formula* has produced. This should show you another weakness of this formula as an attempt to give all the prime numbers. What is the weakness?

The Internet has lots of useful information on prime numbers. Use **Yahoo** to search.

Investigating primes

No one has yet found a formula to check if a particular number is prime.

The following test was found in a Chinese document:

If you want to test whether 3 is prime:
- **first raise 2 to the power of 3, i.e. 2^3, to get 8;**
- **then subtract 2, i.e. $2^3 - 2$, to get 6;**
- **then see if the answer is exactly divisible by 3;**
- **if it is then 3 is prime; if it is not, then it is not.**

Test this rule with five numbers to show that they are prime and five to show that they are not.

It has been shown that for all known primes:

(a) every even number greater than 4 is the sum of two primes (e.g. 8 = 5 + 3, 30 = 17 + 13);

and

(b) every sufficiently large odd number is the sum of three prime numbers (e.g. 37 = 3 + 5 + 29 and 43 = 3 + 17 + 23).

1 Show that these rules work by trying at least five examples of your own for each statement.

....

....

....

....

....

We can write some prime numbers as the sum of two square numbers, e.g. $13 = 2^2 + 3^2$, $5 = 2^2 + 1^2$.

2 Find as many such numbers between 2 and 200 as you can.

....

....

Investigating primes

A twin prime is a set of two consecutive odd primes, e.g. 3, 5.

3 Find all the twin primes less than 101.

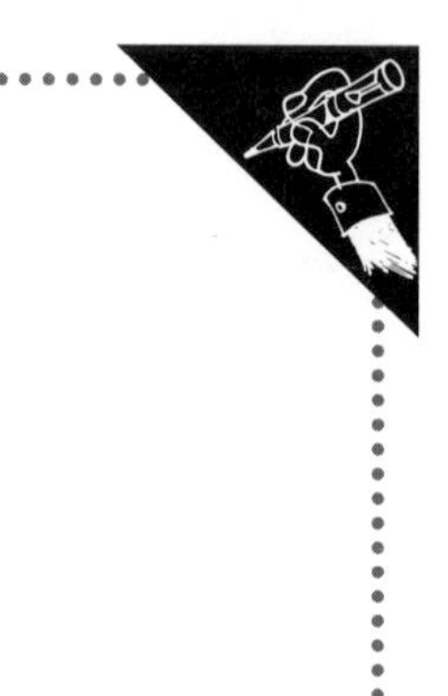

4 Find examples to show that if $2^n - 1$ is a prime, then n must also be a prime. (For example, $2^5 - 1 = 31$: 31 is prime, so is 5.)

Divisibility

1 Look at the following numbers. Without calculating, can you tell which numbers can be divided exactly by 2, 3 or 5?

245, 510, 744, 945, 963, 1185

245 is divisible by ....

510 is divisible by ....

744 is divisible by ....

945 is divisible by ....

963 is divisible by ....

1185 is divisible by ....

2 Complete the following table:

Number	Last digit	Last two digits	Sum of digits	Divisible by 2?	Divisible by 3?	Divisible by 4?	Divisible by 5?	Divisible by 9?	Divisible by 10?
26	6	26	8	Yes	No	No	No	No	No
32	2	32	5	Yes	No	Yes	No	No	No
358	8	58	16	Yes	No	No	No	No	No
40									
51									
54									
73									
78									
490									
519									
585									
745									
771									
879									
4608									
4689									

Divisibility

3 Write down any rules you know for divisibility by 2, by 3, by 4, by 5 and by 9.

4 Ask your neighbour to give you ten numbers to test out your rules.

5 Now experiment to see if you can find rules for 7 and 11 by trying these numbers:

255, 504, 198, 649, 1092, 3531, 286, 336, 504, 1694

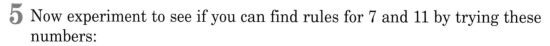

ENTER
SQUARE NUMBER

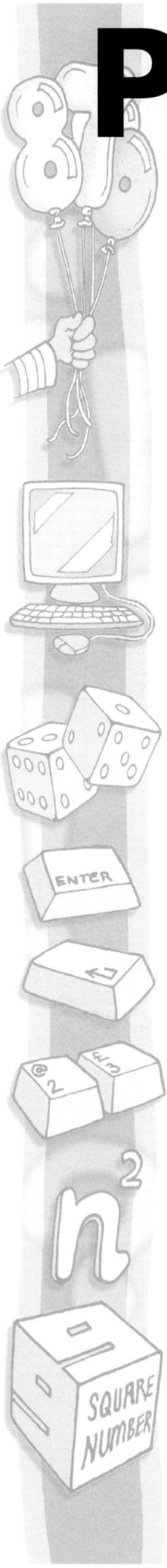

Patterns of numbers in triangles

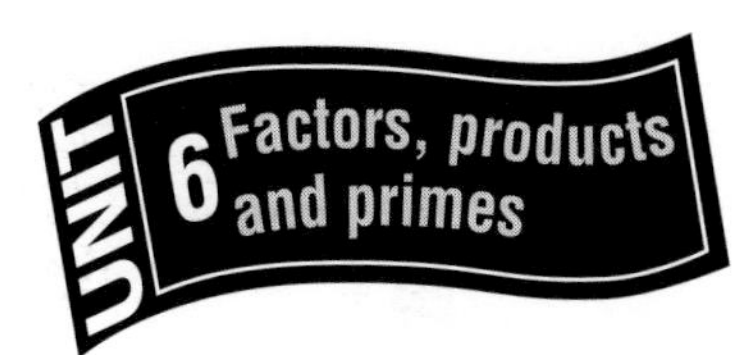

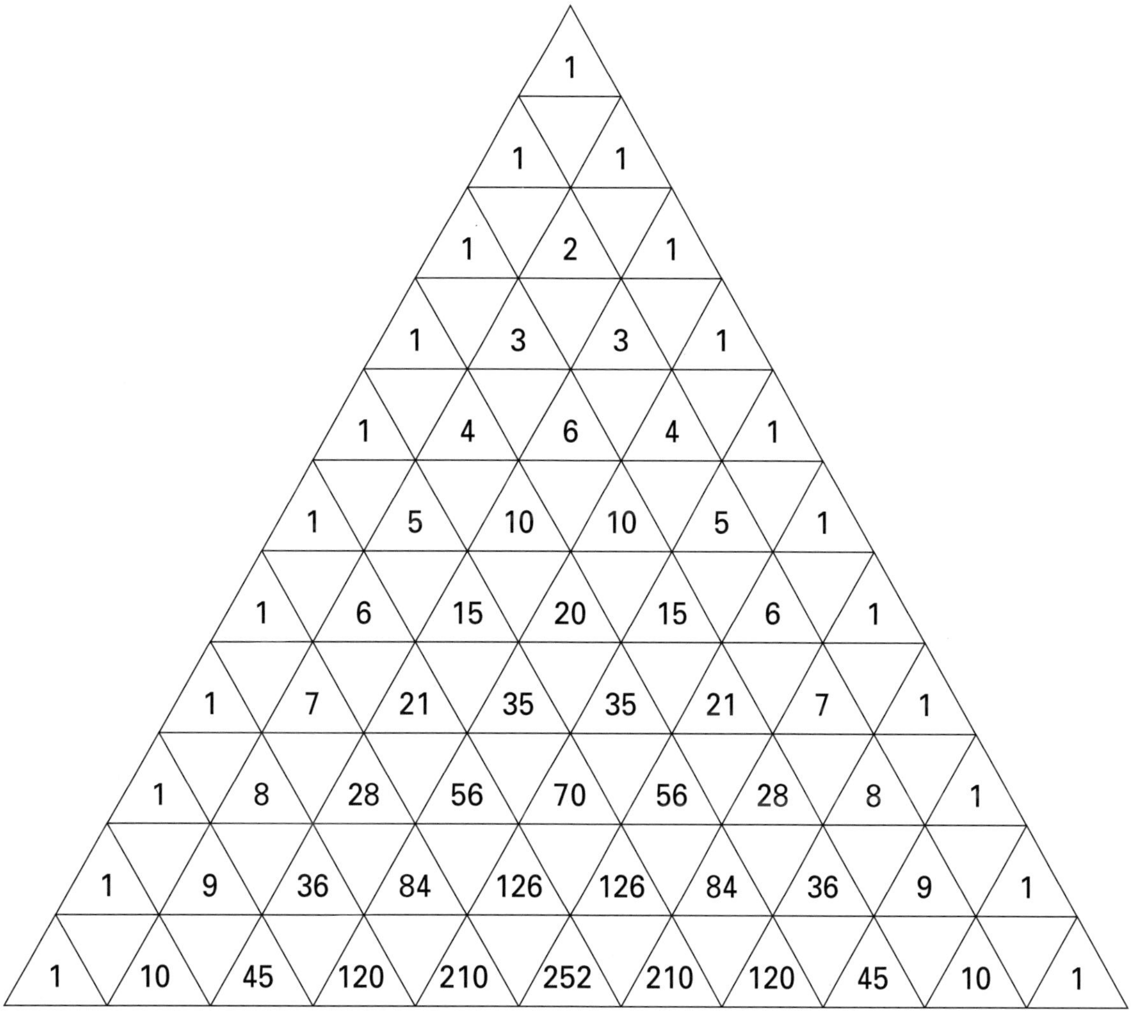

1
1 1
1 2 1
1 3 3 1
1 4 6 4 1
1 5 10 10 5 1
1 6 15 20 15 6 1
1 7 21 35 35 21 7 1
1 8 28 56 70 56 28 8 1
1 9 36 84 126 126 84 36 9 1
1 10 45 120 210 252 210 120 45 10 1

1–100 grids

1	2	3	4	5	6	7	8	9	10
11	12	13	14	15	16	17	18	19	20
21	22	23	24	25	26	27	28	29	30
31	32	33	34	35	36	37	38	39	40
41	42	43	44	45	46	47	48	49	50
51	52	53	54	55	56	57	58	59	60
61	62	63	64	65	66	67	68	69	70
71	72	73	74	75	76	77	78	79	80
81	82	83	84	85	86	87	88	89	90
91	92	93	94	95	96	97	98	99	100

1	2	3	4	5	6	7	8	9	10
11	12	13	14	15	16	17	18	19	20
21	22	23	24	25	26	27	28	29	30
31	32	33	34	35	36	37	38	39	40
41	42	43	44	45	46	47	48	49	50
51	52	53	54	55	56	57	58	59	60
61	62	63	64	65	66	67	68	69	70
71	72	73	74	75	76	77	78	79	80
81	82	83	84	85	86	87	88	89	90
91	92	93	94	95	96	97	98	99	100

Patterns in number

Main focus

To explore and record patterns and relationships in shapes and numbers

Content

Recognising, extending and relating patterns in shapes and numbers

Describing relationships in words and symbols

Notes for teachers

These activities are best approached through an initial class discussion.

Discuss suggestions from pupils about the way they see patterns growing.

It is important that pupils meet the same relationships in different contexts and mediums.

The results of these activities provide a good opportunity for pupils to extend their mathematical language and develop generalisations.

Teachers can help this process by discussing pupils' rules and helping them refine their statements.

Where appropriate, pupils should be encouraged to use symbols to describe the rules.

Pupils could be asked to display their rules.

Learning outcomes

The pupils are able to:

- recognise and predict patterns;
- explain patterns used;
- identify patterns in number sequences;
- state generalisations in words and symbols.

Evaluation

Could the pupils:

- spot and extend the pattern and shapes?
- translate the patterns into numbers?
- record systematically?
- extend the number sequences?
- explain the relationship in words?
- write the rules in words without ambiguity?
- express rules using notation and symbols?

Further activity

Pupils could be asked to construct their own patterns and write down their own rules. It is useful to ask them to discuss their patterns with others and modify their work if necessary.

After the 'Number sequences' activity, pupils could be asked to find out about Lucas sequences, Fibonacci sequences and Golden Ratio (since in both sequences each term is the sum of the two previous terms and the ratio of successive terms tends to the Golden Ratio as a limit).

Resources

Pupil task sheets; square dotted paper

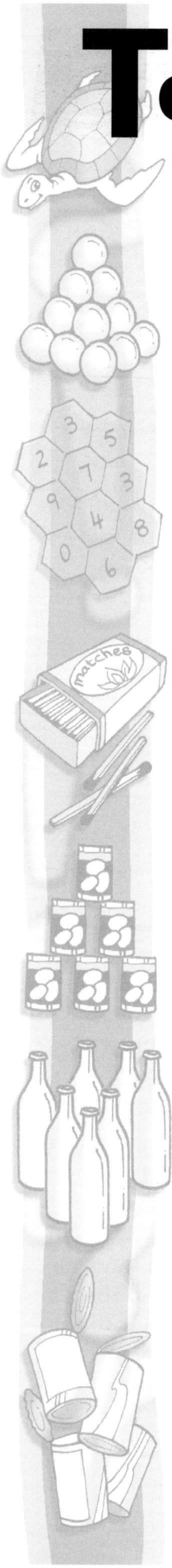

Tower of tins

A supermarket assistant was asked to make a display of baked bean tins. The display has to be ten tins high.

First arrangement

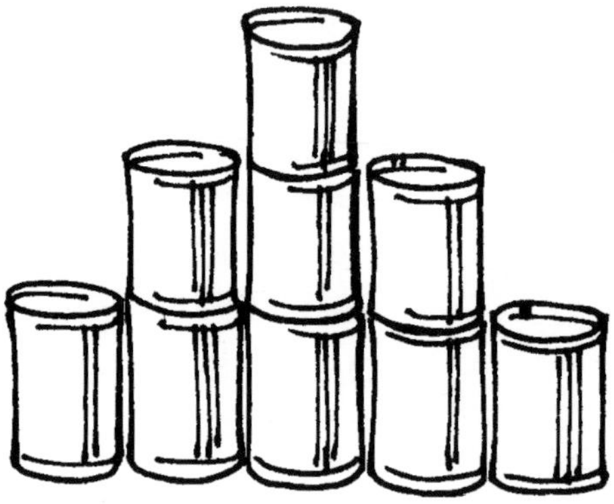

1 How many tins are needed altogether?

....

2 Can you find out how many tins will be on the bottom row?

....

3 Can you predict how many tins would be needed for the bottom row of the model which is 15 tins high (15th model)?

....

4 What about the bottom row of the 20th model?

....

5 Write down a rule for the bottom row of the *n*th model, where *n* can be any number.

....

Second arrangement

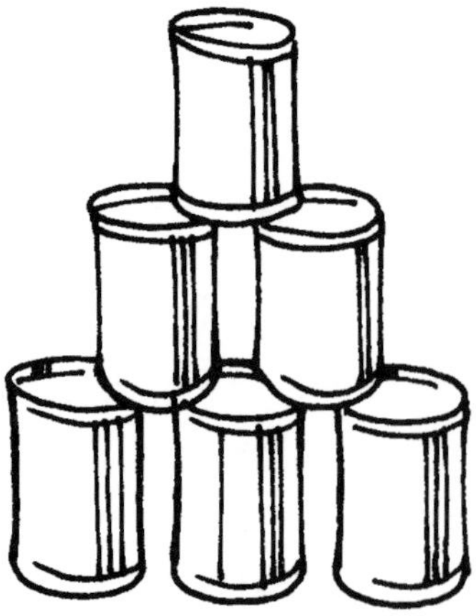

6 If the display was built like this, how many tins would be needed this time?

....

7 How many tins would be on the bottom row of the 10th model?

....

8 Can you spot any patterns?

....

....

....

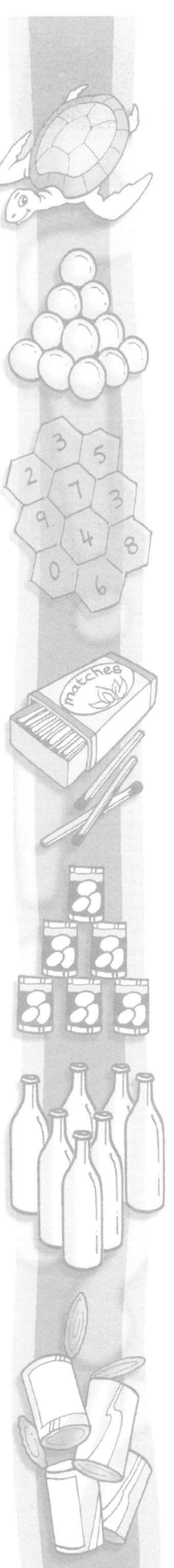

Tower of tins

9 Can you predict how many tins would be needed for the bottom row of the 15th model?

....

10 What about the bottom row of the 20th model?

....

11 Write down a rule for the bottom row of the *n*th model, where *n* can be any number.

....

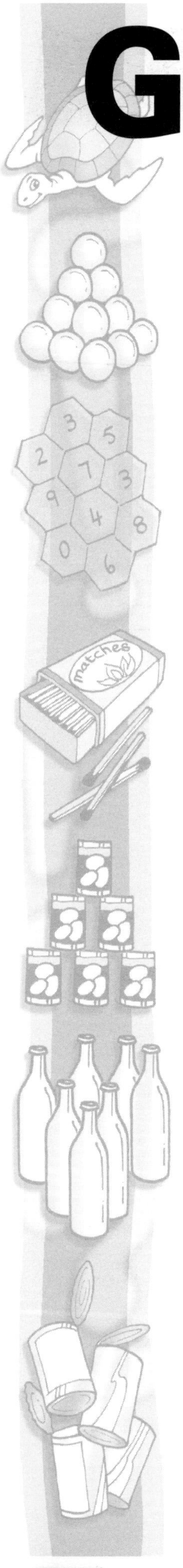

Growth patterns

UNIT 7 Patterns in number

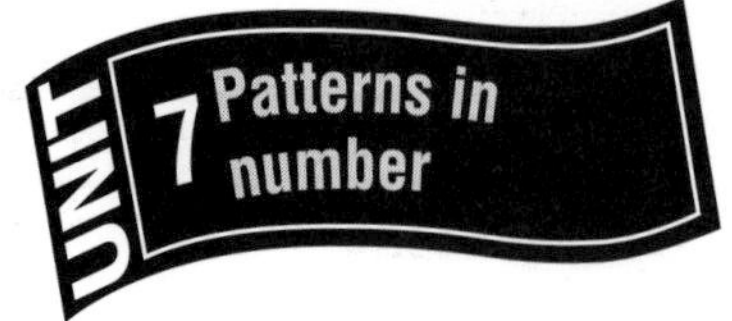

Look at this pattern.

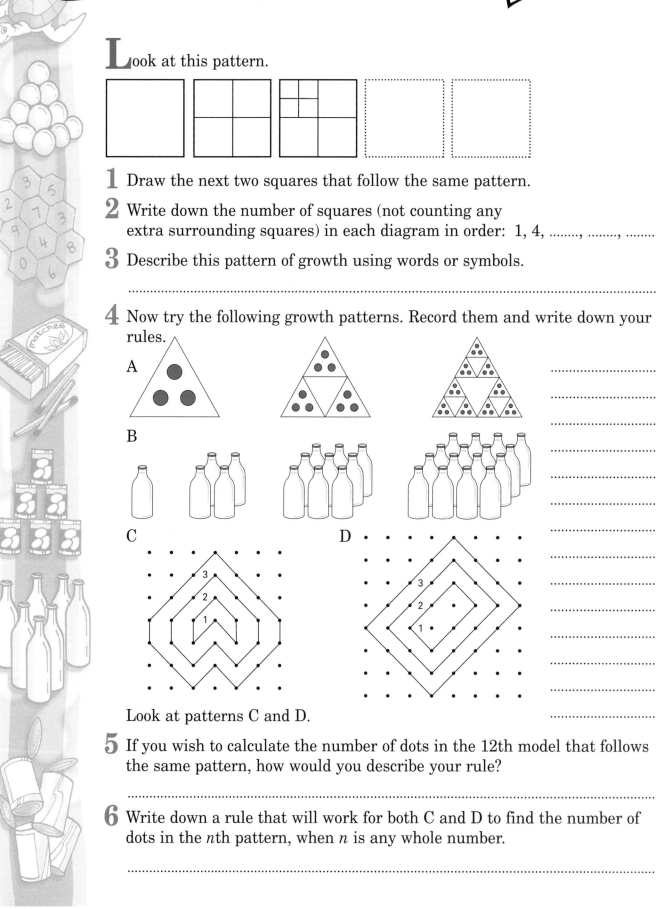

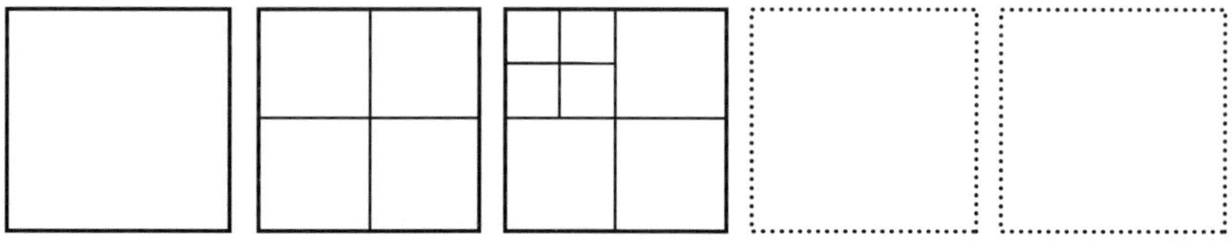

1 Draw the next two squares that follow the same pattern.

2 Write down the number of squares (not counting any extra surrounding squares) in each diagram in order: 1, 4, ..., ..., ...

3 Describe this pattern of growth using words or symbols.

....

4 Now try the following growth patterns. Record them and write down your rules.

A

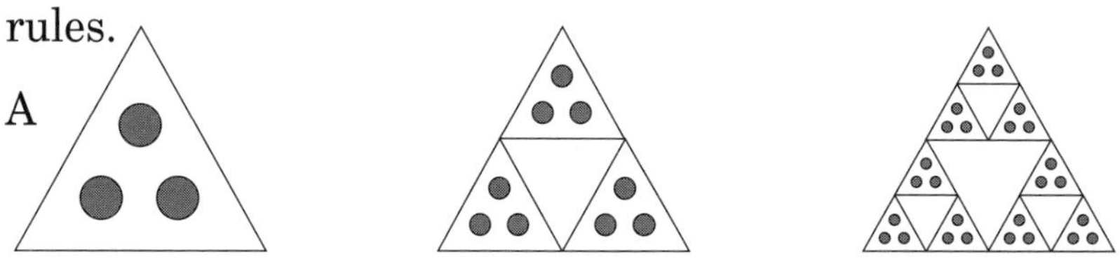

B

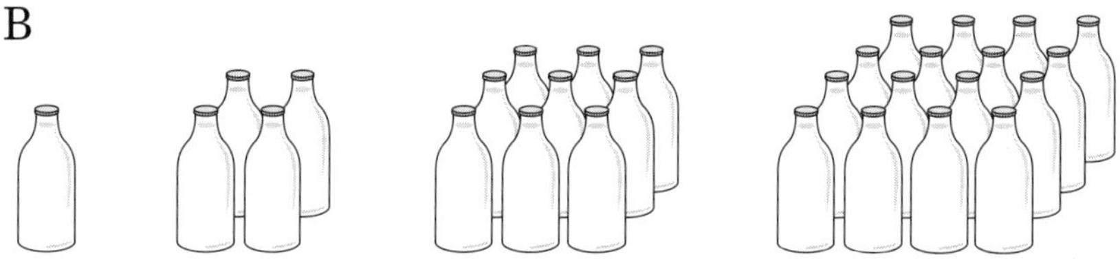

C

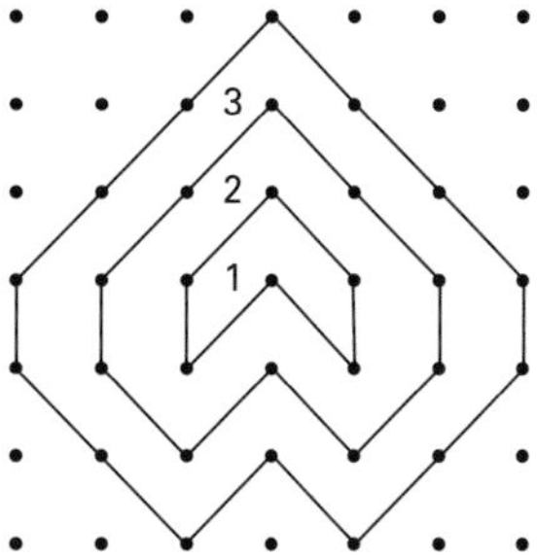

D

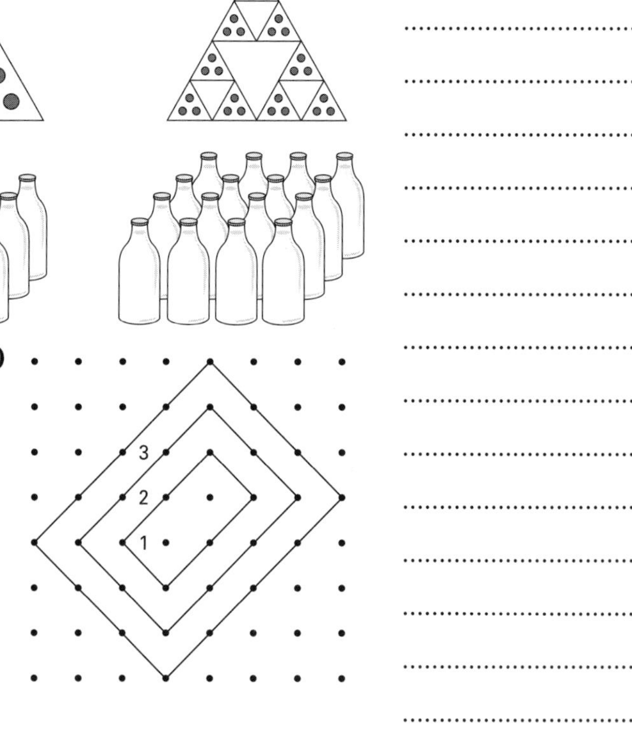

Look at patterns C and D.

5 If you wish to calculate the number of dots in the 12th model that follows the same pattern, how would you describe your rule?

....

6 Write down a rule that will work for both C and D to find the number of dots in the *n*th pattern, when *n* is any whole number.

....

Number sequences

1 Find the next two numbers in the sequence below and write down your rule.

3, 5, 8, 13, 21, ..., ...

....

2 Using your rule, find the missing numbers in the following sequences.

1		4				29

3				18

8				52

2					41

3 Make up five of your own sequence problems, using different first and last numbers and different lengths of sequences. Describe how you made them up.

Stacking cannonballs

4 Cannonballs can be stacked in a variety of ways. The diagram shows how they can be arranged in triangular and square layers. Find, for each one, the number of balls in each layer and the totals for two, three and four layers.

Square Triangular

....

....

5 Calculate the number of balls in the 10th layer for each arrangement. What would be the total number of balls in each case? Describe your rules.

....

....

....

....

Patterns of numbers

The Greeks and Romans used pebbles to help them with numbers. The word for pebble was **calculus**, which gives us our word **calculate** and a branch of mathematics called **calculus**, which you may meet in the Sixth Form.

They found it helpful to arrange the pebbles in patterns. We still use these patterns on dice, dominoes and playing cards.

We talk about **square numbers**:

triangular numbers:

and **rectangular numbers**:

If a number cannot be arranged as a **rectangular number** it is a **prime number**.

1 Megan looked at the pattern for 5 on a die: and decided that  would be better.

Can you explain why she suggested that?

....

....

Look at how the pattern of square numbers grows:

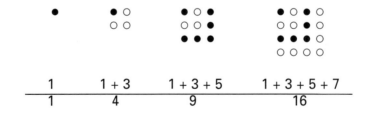

1	1 + 3	1 + 3 + 5	1 + 3 + 5 + 7
1	4	9	16

2 Continue the sequence for the square numbers 25, 36, 49.

Patterns of numbers

3 Complete the following statements:

The first square number is the first odd number.

(a) The second square number is the sum of the first .... consecutive odd numbers.

(b) The third square number is the sum of the first .... consecutive odd numbers.

(c) The fourth square number is the sum of the first .... consecutive odd numbers.

4 Predict the following:

(a) The tenth square number is the sum of the first .... consecutive odd numbers.

(b) The nth square number is the sum of the first .... consecutive odd numbers.

5 **(a)** Find the sum of the first 20 consecutive odd numbers – *without adding them up!*

....

(b) Find the sum of the first 20 consecutive numbers.

....

(c) How many consecutive odd numbers give a sum of 1024?

....

6 Give a formula for finding the value of the nth square number.

....

Triangular numbers

Here is the pattern for triangular numbers:

1	1 + 2	1 + 2 + 3	1 + 2 + 3 + 4	1 + 2 + 3 + 4 + 5
1	3	6	10	15
Δ_1	Δ_2	Δ_3	Δ_4	Δ_5

Δ_1 is short for 'first triangular number', Δ_2 for 'second triangular number', etc.

The sequence 1 + 2 + 3 + 4 + 5 could be described as the sum of the first five **consecutive numbers**.

1 Complete the following statements:

(a) The third triangular number is the sum of the first .... consecutive numbers.
(b) The fourth triangular number is the sum of the first .... consecutive numbers.
(c) The tenth triangular number is the sum of the first .... consecutive numbers.
(d) The nth triangular number is the sum of the first .... consecutive numbers.

Unlike **square numbers**, where there is an obvious formula for the nth square number = n^2, the one for **triangular numbers** is not so obvious and has to be found.

Rory noticed this pattern by putting two copies of the same triangular number together:

$2 \times \Delta_2 = 2 \times 3$ $\quad 2 \times \Delta_3 = 3 \times 4$ $\quad 2 \times \Delta_4 = 4 \times 5$ $\quad 2 \times \Delta_5 = 5 \times 6$

2 If you continue this pattern, write down the following:

(a) $2 \times \Delta_7 =$ .... **(b)** $2 \times \Delta_{11} =$ .... **(c)** $2 \times \Delta_n$ ....

Triangular numbers

Rory then wrote his formula like this: $\Delta_3 = \dfrac{3 \times 4}{2}$

3 Do the same for these:

(a) $2 \times \Delta_4 = 4 \times 5$ means $\Delta_4 =$ ....

(b) $2 \times \Delta_{11} = 11 \times 12$ means $\Delta_{11} =$ ....

(c) $2 \times \Delta_n =$ .... means $\Delta_n =$ ...., which is the formula for triangular numbers.

4 Use this formula to find Δ_{20}, Δ_{45}, Δ_{100}, and the sum of the first 20 consecutive numbers.

....

....

....

....

5 In the nineteenth century an 8-year-old boy amazed his teacher by using the method shown below to find the sum of the first 100 consecutive numbers. His name was Gauss and he became one of the most famous mathematicians of the century.

1	2	3	4	5	6	7	....	96	97	98	99	100	
100	99	98	97	96	95	94	....	5	4	3	2	1	+
101	101	101	101	101	101	101		101	101	101	101	101	

Can you complete his calculation? Check, using your formula.

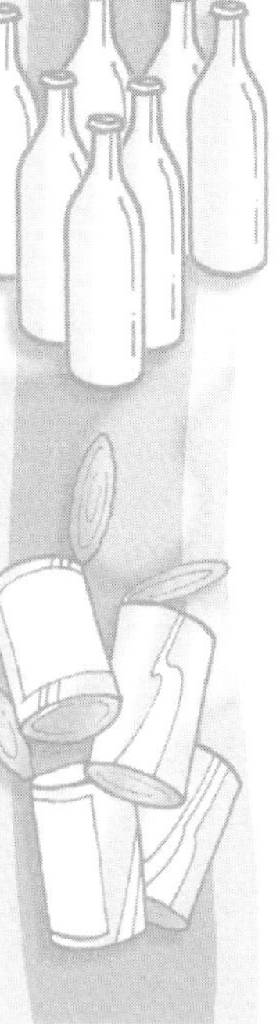

How do your triangles grow?

Here we have some triangles made from matchsticks. There are matchsticks making the outside of the triangle and dividing the triangle into triangles of side 1 matchstick.

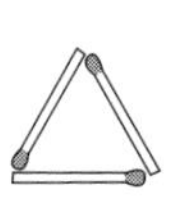

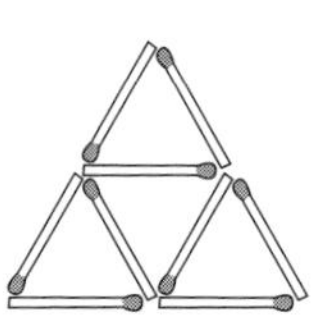

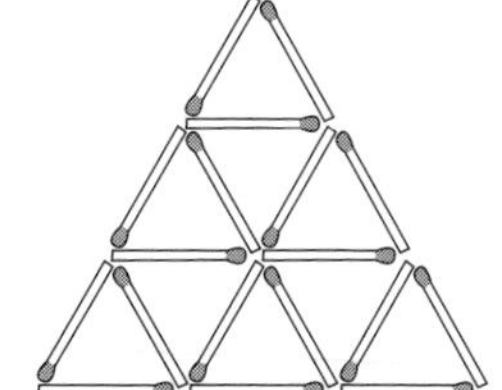

Study this table:

Side of triangle	Outside	Inside	Total
1	3	0	3
2	6	3	9
3	9	9	18
4	12	18	30

1 Look at the 'Outside' column. Explain the pattern of numbers.

....

....

2 Predict the value for a triangle of side 6 matchsticks.

....

3 Give a formula for the number of outside matchsticks for a triangle of side 20 matchsticks.

....

4 Give a formula for the number of outside matchsticks for a triangle of side n.

....

5 Draw a triangle of side 5 on the isometric dotted paper provided, and count the outside and inside matchstick totals.

Outside: ....

Inside: ....

Look at the totals column, i.e. 3, 9, 18, 30. Did you notice that the numbers are all multiples of 3? So we can write the numbers as 3 × (1, 3, 6, 10, 15, 21, ...).

6 Do you recognise the number sequence 1, 3, 6, 10, 15, 21? What type of numbers are they? The 'Triangular numbers' task sheet will help.

....

How do your triangles grow?

7 Use your knowledge of this sequence to predict the values for the table below.

Side of triangle	Outside	Inside	Total
5			
6			
7			
12			

8 *Challenge question:* find a formula for the 'total' column.

....

The first magic square?

Kate was doing a project on magic squares and decided to search the Internet at school using the 'Alta Vista' search engine. (You may have met magic squares before: the columns, rows and diagonals add up to the same total – the 'magic number'.) On a Web page by Suzanne Alejandre, Kate found the following drawing based on the legend of Lo Shu from about 3000 years ago.

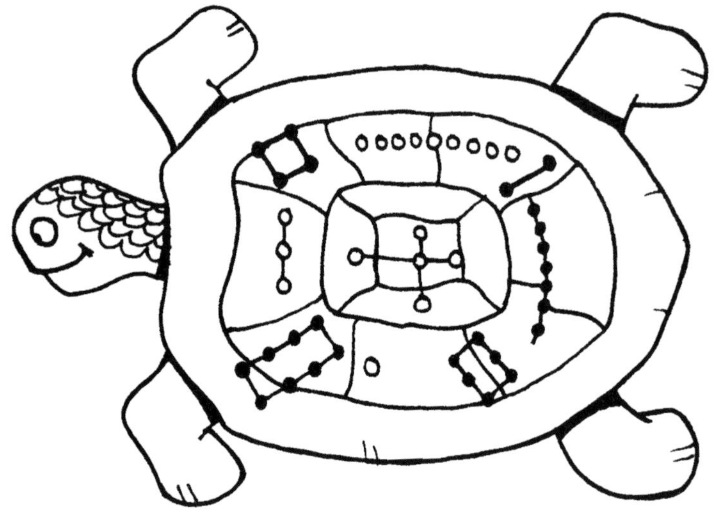

Suzanne Alejandre quotes the story as follows:

> In the ancient time of China, there was a huge flood. The people tried to offer some sacrifice to the 'river god' of one of the flooding rivers, the Lo River, to calm his anger. However, each time a turtle came from the river and walked around the sacrifice. The river god did not accept the sacrifice until one time, a child noticed the curious figure on the turtle shell. Hence they realised the correct amount of sacrifice to make.

Use the 3 × 3 grid below to make a more familiar magic square. The top row has already been completed. Finish off the magic square and give the magic number.

4	9	2

Number patterns 1

Magic squares

In the year 1514, a famous German artist named Albrecht Dürer published an engraving called *Melancholia*, which included the following array of numbers:

16	3	2	13
5	10	11	8
9	6	7	12
4	15	14	1

1 Check that this is a magic square.

2 What is the magic number? ....

3 You can rearrange the magic square by rotations and reflections. Give one example of each on the 4×4 grids below.

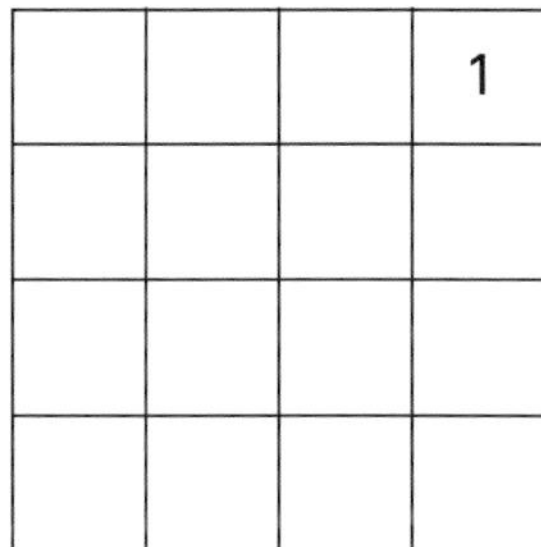

			1

Rotation

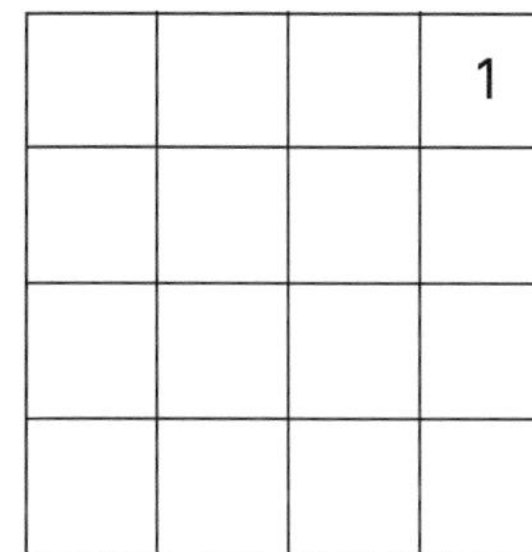

			1

Reflection

4 Why do you think that Dürer chose the pattern of numbers shown at the top rather than a rotation or reflection?

....

....

Number patterns 2

UNIT 7 Patterns in number

Franklin squares

Benjamin Franklin (1706–90) invented this variation on a magic square. In this case the sum of the diagonals does not give the magic number (which is 260), but many other patterns of eight numbers do.

52	61	4	13	20	29	36	45
14	3	62	51	46	35	30	19
53	60	5	12	21	28	37	44
11	6	59	54	43	38	27	22
55	58	7	10	23	26	39	42
9	8	57	56	41	40	25	24
50	63	2	15	18	31	34	47
16	1	64	49	48	33	32	17

For example, check the following patterns on the square above for a sum of 260:

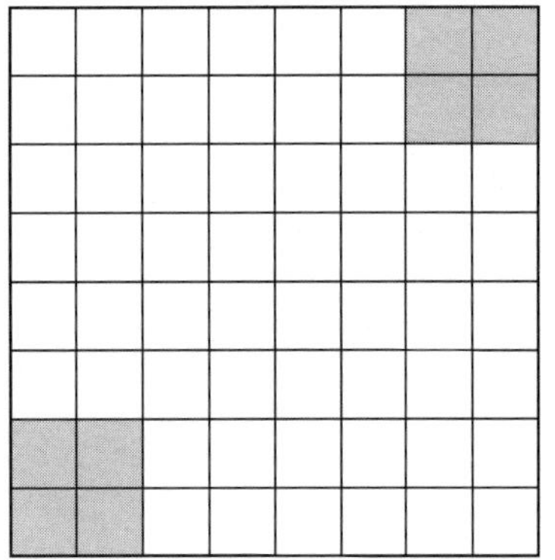

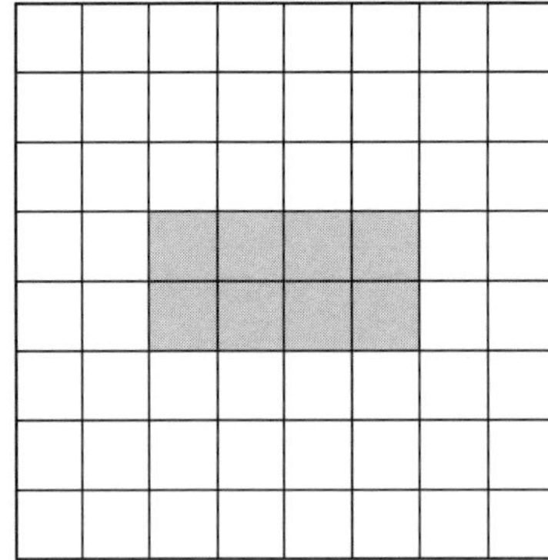

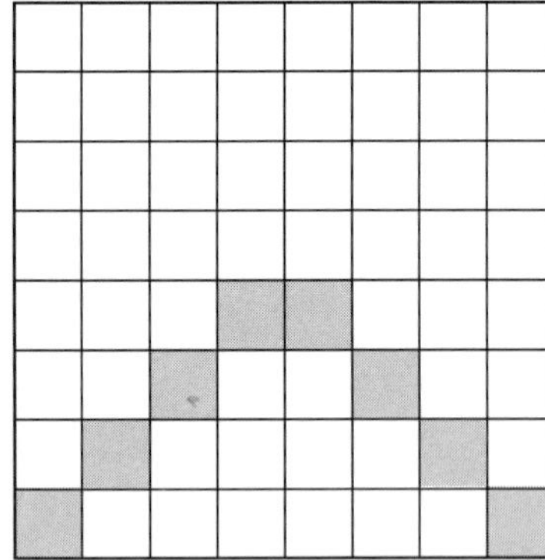

Try other combinations of eight squares and mark the ones that work on the Franklin squares sheet provided.

Franklin squares

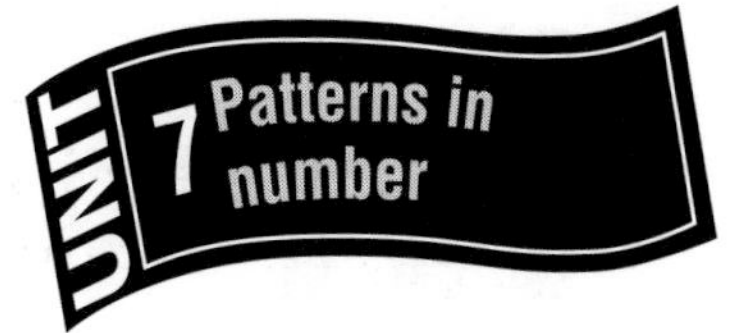

Mark the patterns that make 260.

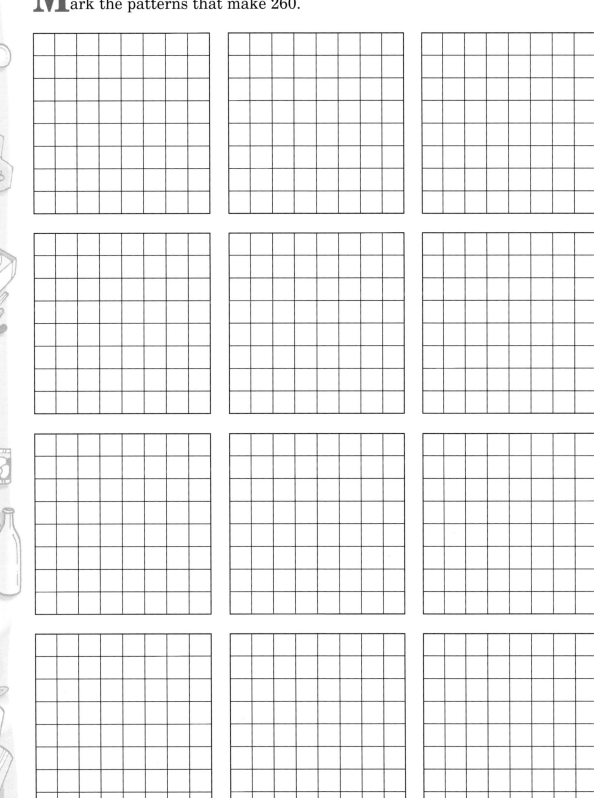

Magic squares and other shapes

You will already have come across magic squares on previous task sheets. Now look at this one:

17	89	71
113	59	5
47	29	101

1 Check that it is a magic square (columns, rows and diagonals should add up to the same totals).

2 What is the magic number? ....

3 Look at the nine numbers on the grid. What kind of numbers are they? (Apart from the fact that they are all odd – you need to go further than that!)

....

Here is a 4 × 4 grid:

101	47	31	79
73	61	71	53
43	67	59	89
41	83	97	37

4 Find the magic number. ....

5 The numbers in the grid are all prime numbers. List them in ascending order (31, 37, etc.).

....

....

....

....

6 Look at the list of prime numbers on the 'Prime numbers 2 – using a spreadsheet' task sheet (pp. 65–6). Mark your numbers on the list. What do you notice?

....

....

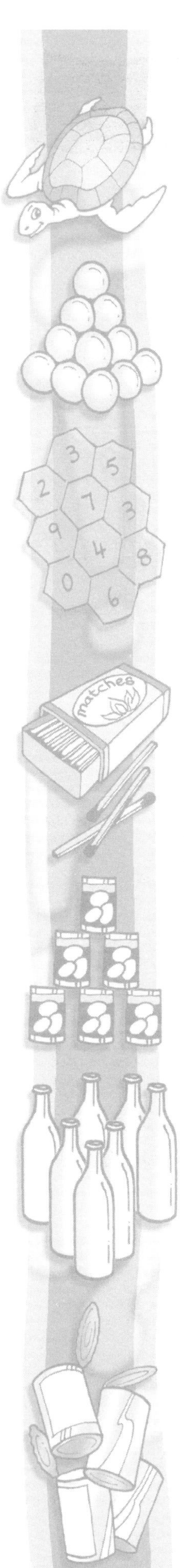

Magic squares and other shapes

On a Web site, a Professor Mutsumi Suzuki lists the following 3 × 3 magic square, made up of prime numbers:

409	1879	829
1459	1039	619
1249	199	1669

7 Check that it is a magic square.

8 Find the magic number. ....

9 List the prime numbers in ascending order (199, 409, 619, etc.).

....

....

....

....

10 Check your list to see if they *are* all prime numbers. Is the magic number prime?

11 Look at your list from question 9. Explain why these particular numbers have been chosen for this magic square. (Apart from the fact that they all end in 9.)

....

....

....

The magic hexagon

Another Web site is headed 'Magic hexagon'. Columns and diagonals all add up to the magic number. Here is a partly completed magic hexagon. Complete it!

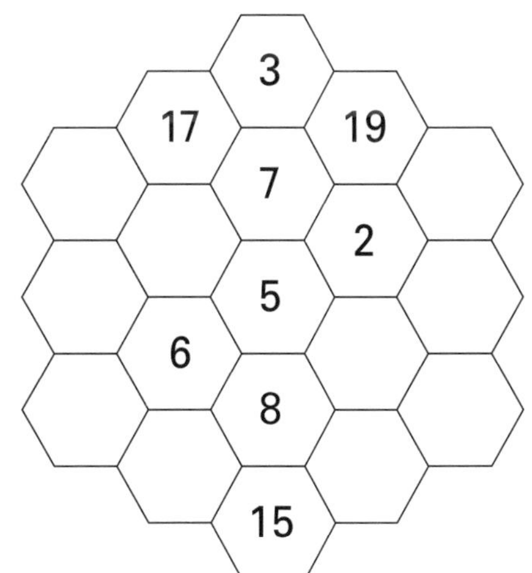

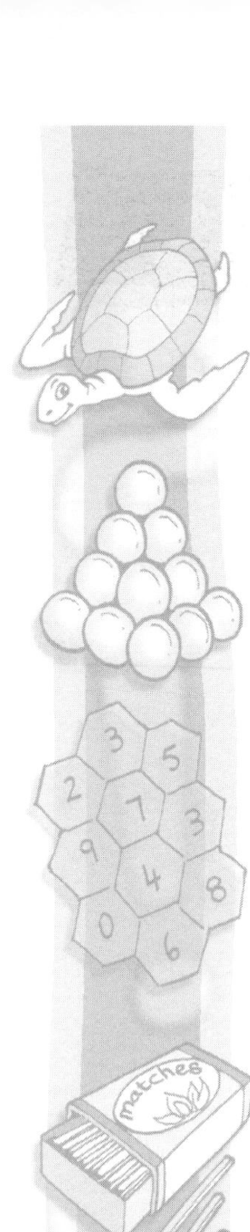

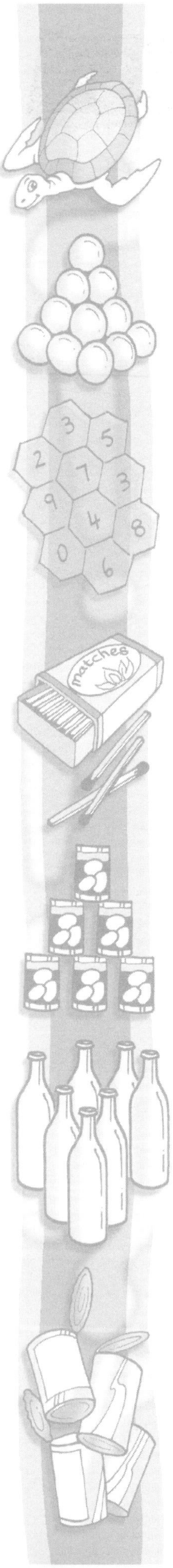

Magic squares and other shapes

UNIT 7 Patterns in number

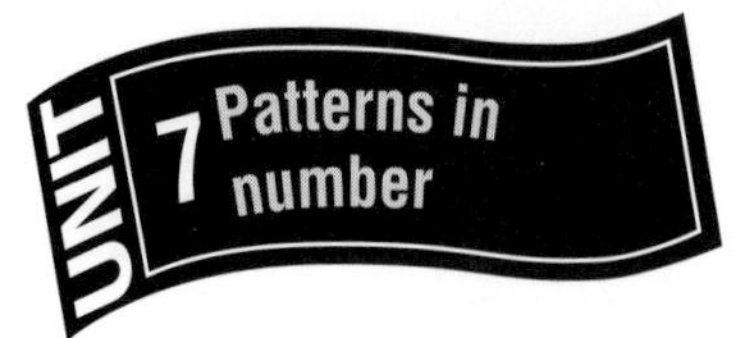

Magic Star of David

The magic star uses the numbers 1 to 12 once and once only. The magic number is the sum of the four numbers on each line. For example, the first one is complete and contains the magic number for all these stars. Fill in the missing numbers on all the others – same magic number, all contain numbers 1 to 12 once and once only.

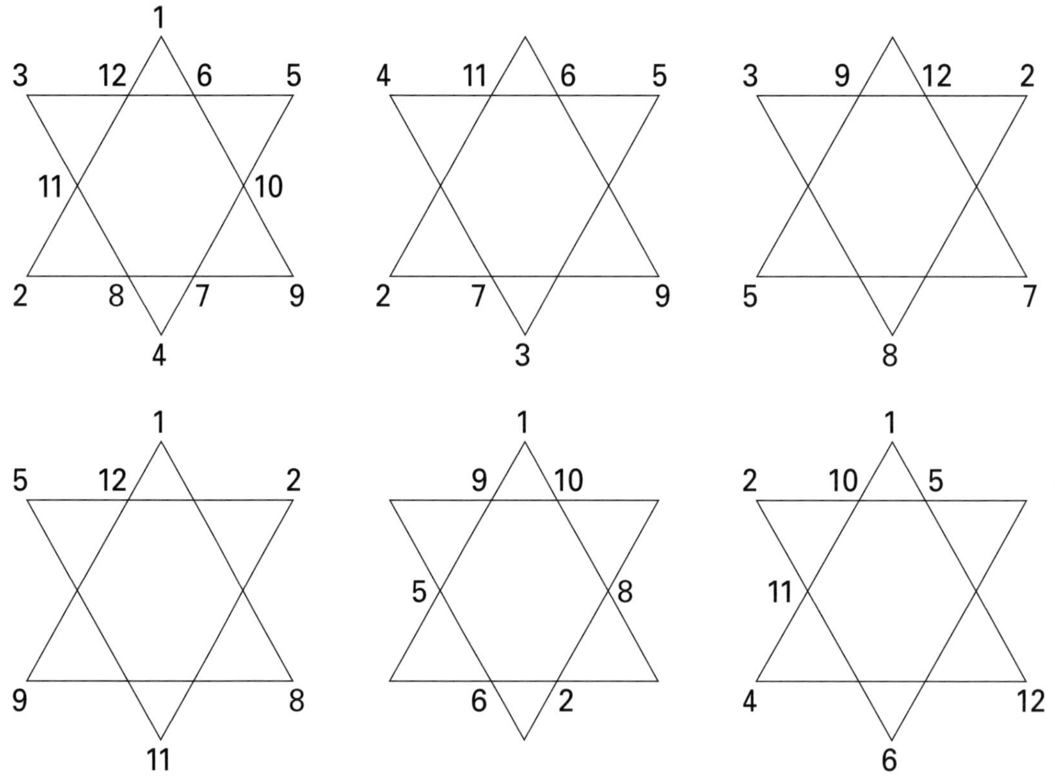

1
3 12 6 5
11 10
2 8 7 9
4
4 11 6 5
2 7 9
3
3 9 12 2
5 7
8
1
5 12 2
9 8
11
1
9 10
5 8
6 2
1
2 10 5
11
4 12
6

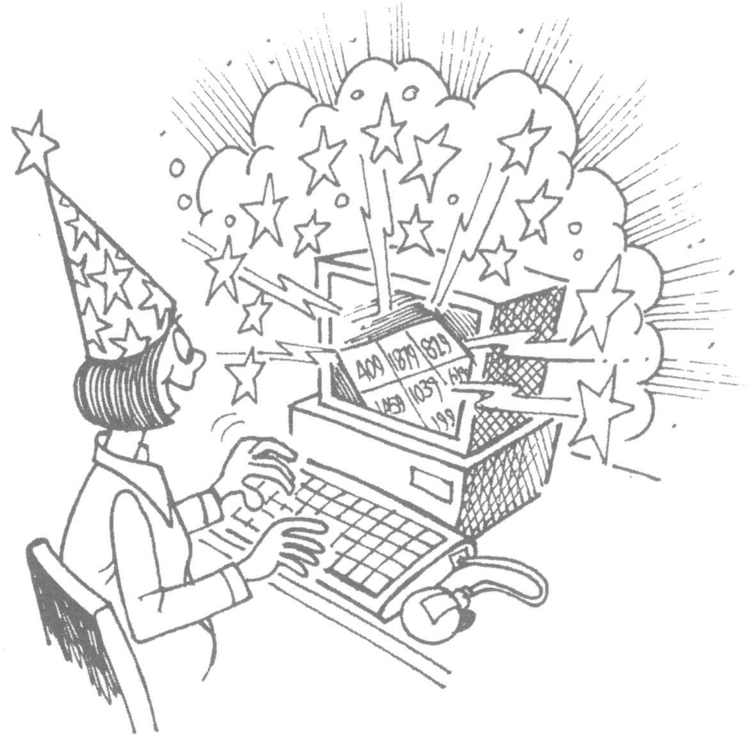

3
5
2
7
3
9
4
8
0
6
matches

Mathematical understanding is improved when pupils are encouraged to describe and record relationships, as well as to discover and create patterns

Think about how to adapt tasks and questions from textbooks, worksheets or test papers, so that pupils can become more involved in making decisions, describing patterns and relationships, and testing conjectures.

Probability

Main focus

Practical and experimental work to help appreciate some of the principles governing random events

Content

Informal investigations of simple ideas of probability

Predicting and evaluating outcomes of experiments

Understanding and using vocabulary and formal representations

Relative frequency

Notes for teachers

At this stage, pupils would have developed a good intuitive understanding of possible and impossible events. They might, however, have difficulty in differentiating between impossible and unlikely events.

It is assumed that pupils have carried out probability experiments such as tossing a coin or rolling a die and compared actual outcomes against expected (theoretical) outcomes.

The activities are designed to promote discussion on outcomes that are not equally likely, as pupils often have a false belief that chances are always 'equal' (for example, coin tossing).

It is important that teachers encourage pupils to refine their language and concepts through discussion and writing and to use formal vocabulary and notation.

Pooling of class results can lead to a better illustration of the ideas.

Learning outcomes

The pupils are able to:

- ◆ appreciate the notion of probability through experience as well as experiment;
- ◆ discuss events and experiments using vocabulary such as 'certain', 'probably', 'likely', 'uncertain', 'fair';
- ◆ record, interpret and represent information using tables, charts, graphs and symbols.

Evaluation

Could the pupils:

- ◆ classify events with understanding?
- ◆ represent and interpret information gathered?
- ◆ use the probability scale sensibly?
- ◆ understand and use associated vocabulary?
- ◆ make sensible observations from the outcomes of experiments?

Further activity

Ask pupils to bring examples of numerical data they use in other subject areas and discuss various approaches to tackling this.

Resources

Spinners; dice; pupil task sheets; calculators; computers

Placing probabilities on the probability line

UNIT 8 Probability

Look at the statements below and work out the probability of the events happening. Cut the statements out and stick them on the probability line at the place where you think they belong.

For example, **Spin a coin and get a HEAD** has a probability of a half or 0.5, and is placed in its correct position on the probability line.

Throw two coins and get two tails

Once in a blue moon

Throw a 6 with a die

Throw a drawing pin and it lands point up

It will go dark tonight

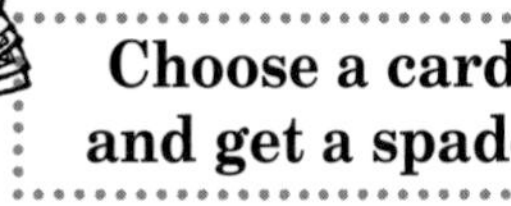

Choose a card and get a spade

Throw a die and get a prime number

See a woman who is 3 metres tall

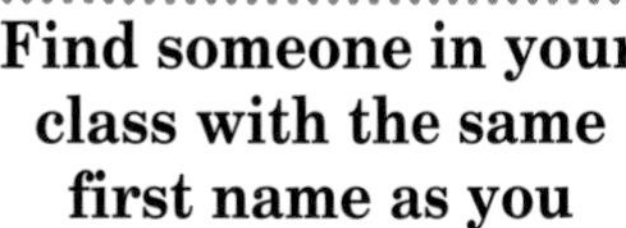

Find someone in your class with the same first name as you

Throw an even number with a die

Choose a year at random and find that it is a leap year

Choose a card and get a red one

Choose a card and get a red king

Choose a card and get an ace

Choose a month at random and find that it has 30 days

Useful information

- A die has six faces.
- A pack of cards has 52 cards in four equal suits – clubs, spades (both black cards), and hearts and diamonds (both red cards).
- The world's tallest woman is Zeng Jinlian of China, at 2.48 metres.

Probability line

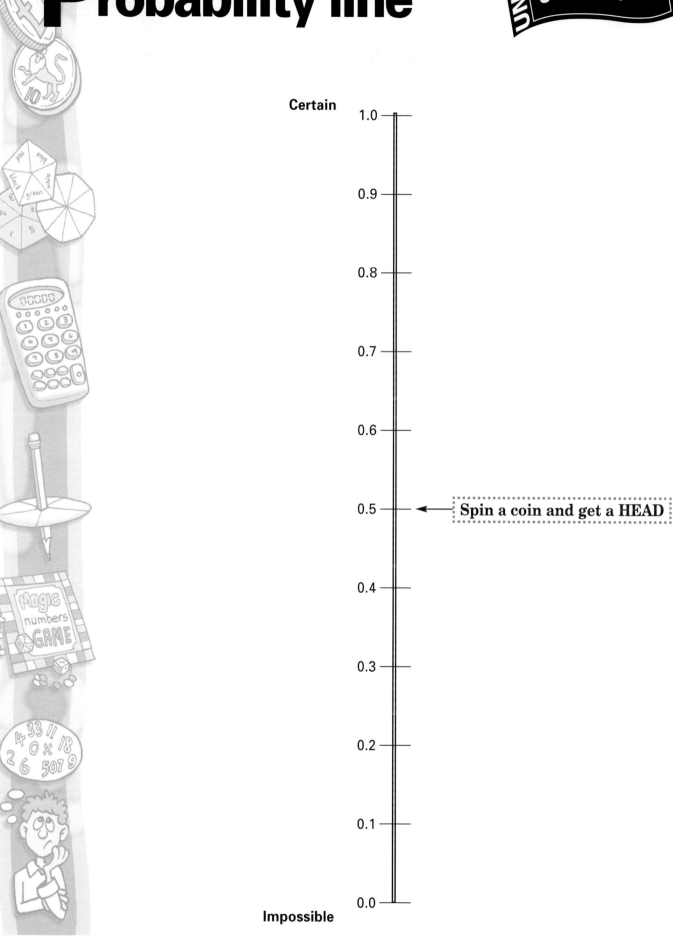

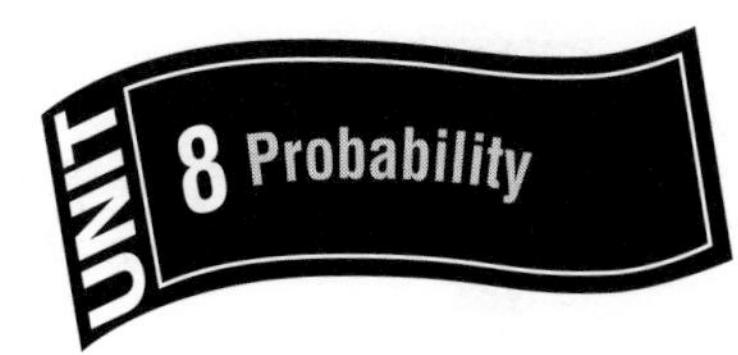

Certain

1.0

0.9

0.8

0.7

0.6

0.5 ← Spin a coin and get a HEAD

0.4

0.3

0.2

0.1

0.0

Impossible

Test your probability power

1 Find the probability of the following events taking place:

(a) An ordinary die thrown once shows a 6.

....

(b) Four ordinary coins tossed together all show the same side.

....

(c) Your first child will be born on a Tuesday.

....

(d) Two ordinary dice thrown together show a total of 9.

....

(e) A whole number chosen at random is a multiple of 5.

....

2 Which of the above events is the most likely?

....

3 Three ordinary dice are thrown one after the other. The first die thrown shows a 3. The second and third dice are then thrown. Calculate, as a fraction, the probability that:

(a) all three dice show the same score ....

(b) all three dice show different scores ....

(c) the sum of the three scores is more than 13 ....

(d) the sum of the three scores is less than 5 ....

(e) the product of the three scores is a prime number ....

Predict and test spinners

Look at the spinners and predict the following probabilities. (Some spinners are provided for you to cut out, on p. 99.)

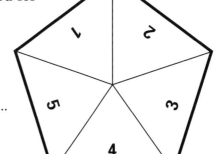

Spinner A

1 2 3 4 5

Spinner A

1 Predict the probability of spinning a 1 (we write p(1)) ....

2 Predict p(3) ....

3 Predict p(even number) ....

4 Predict p(prime number) ....

Spinner B

Red Blue Green Red Black

Spinner B

5 Predict p(green) ....

6 Predict p(red) ....

7 Predict p(not black) ....

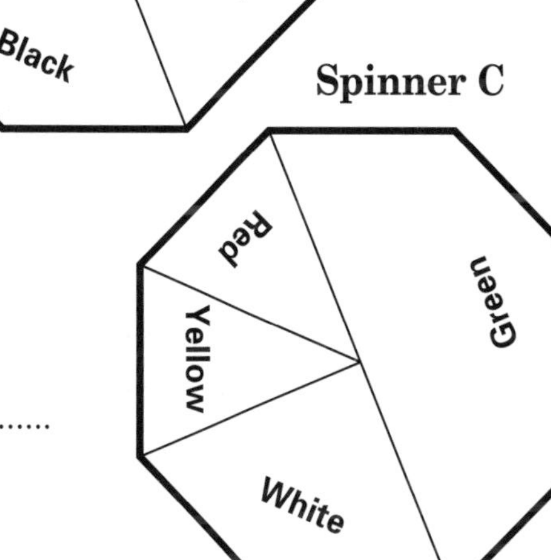

Spinner C

8 Predict p(red) ....

9 What other colour has the same probability as red? ....

10 Predict p(either white or yellow) ....

Spinners D and **E** are for you to make up situations to try on your friends.

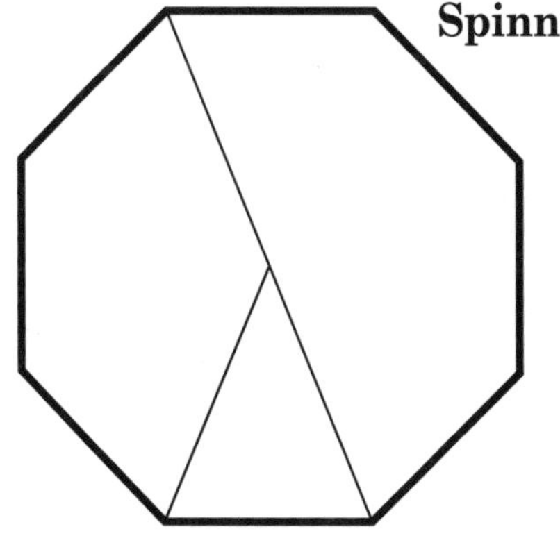

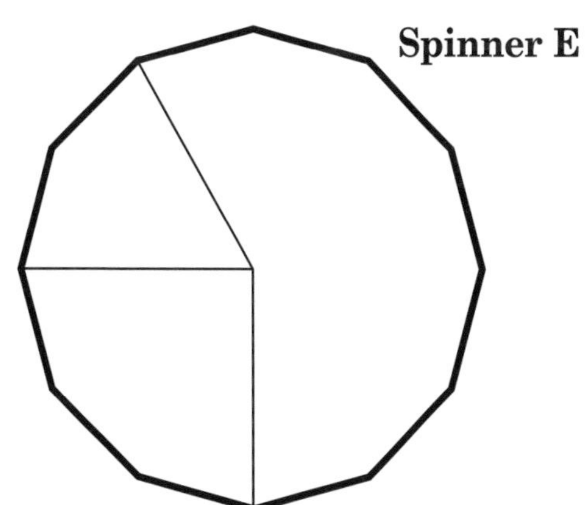

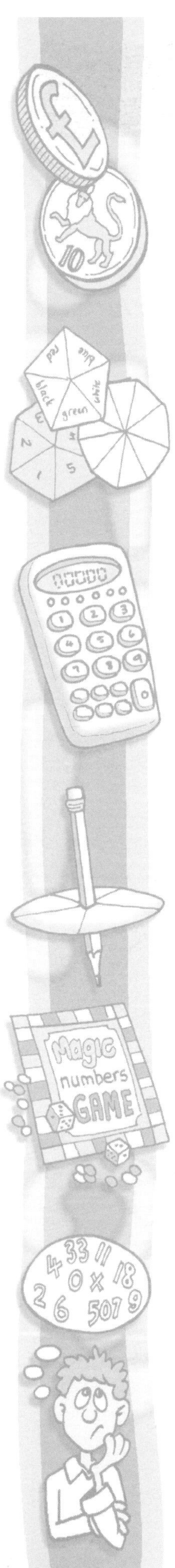

Predict and test spinners

Spinner F

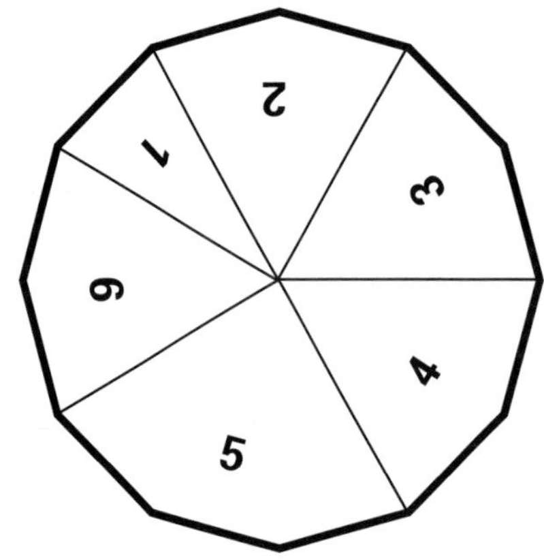

11 Predict p(1), p(2), p(3), p(4), p(5), p(6)

....

....

If this spinner were spun 60 times, predict how many times you would get each of the numbers:

Score	1	2	3	4	5	6
Number						

12 Now test the spinner by spinning it 60 times, and record your scores.

Score	1	2	3	4	5	6
Number						

13 How close are your results to your prediction?

....

14 Combine your results with others in your class. Discuss the group results with your teacher.

Spinners

Spinner A

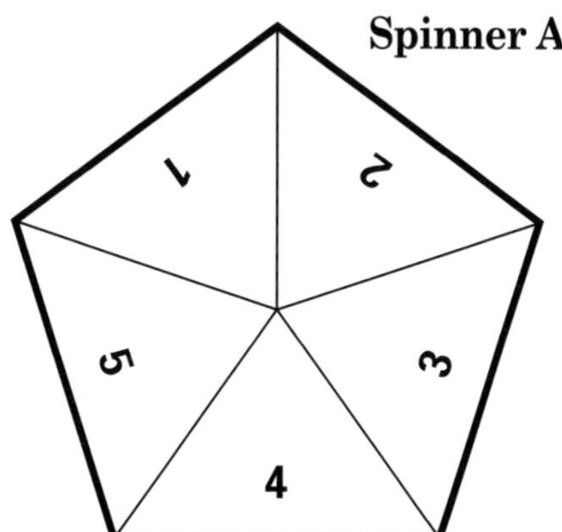

Spinner B

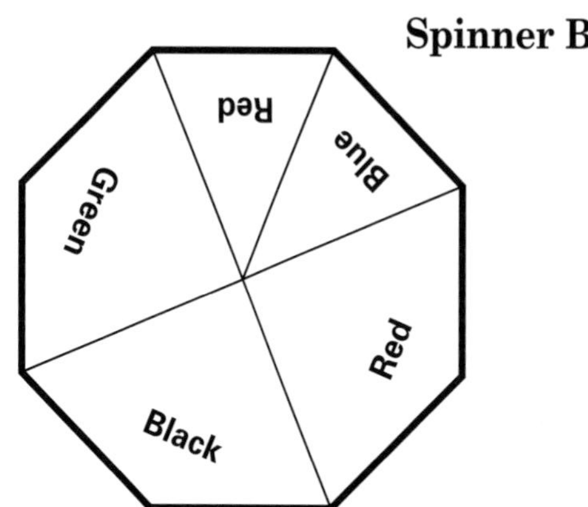

Spinner C

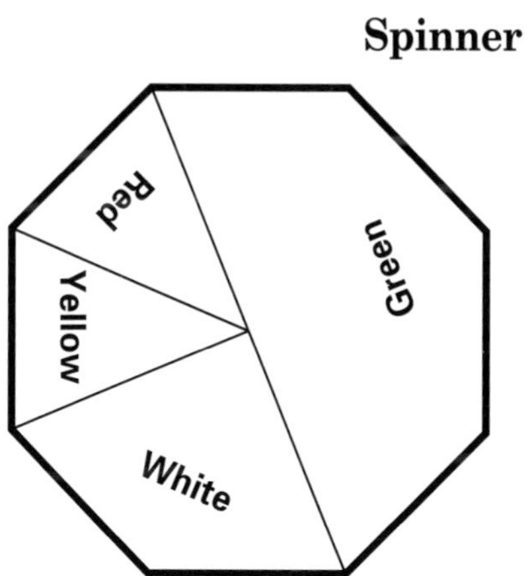

Spinner D

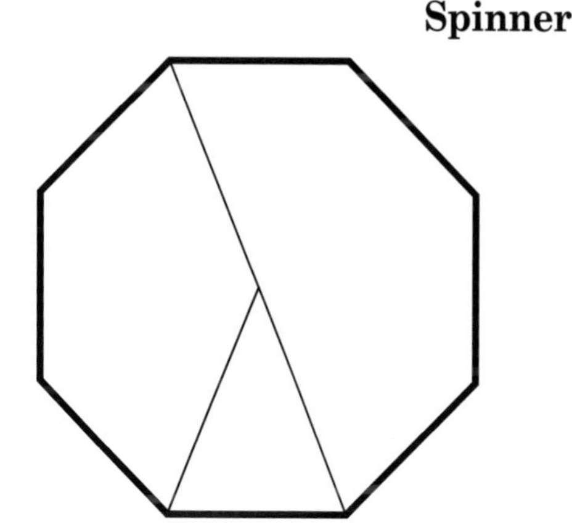

Spinner E

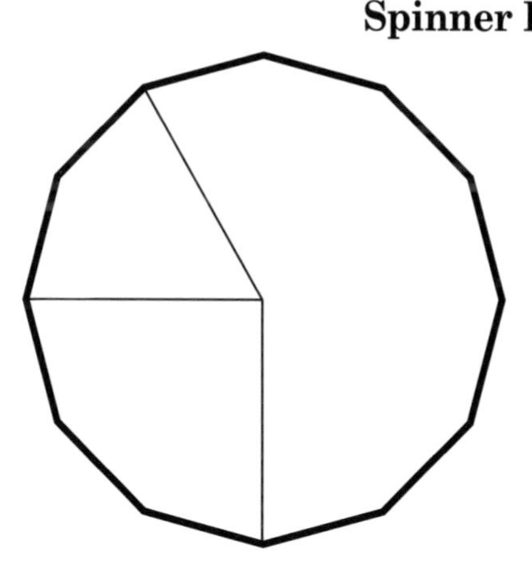

Spinner F

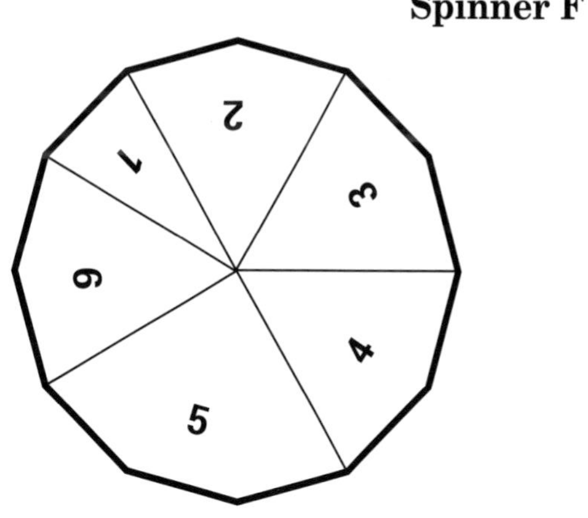

But does it all add up?

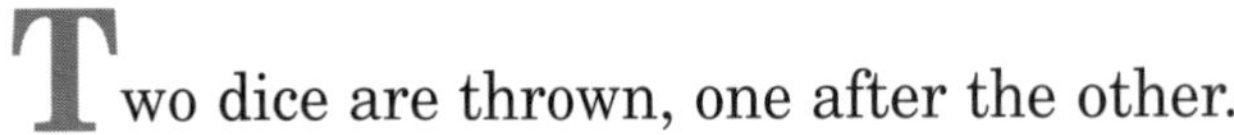

Two dice are thrown, one after the other.

1 Complete the table.

First die (columns), Second die (rows)

+	1	2	3	4	5	6
1	2	3	4	5	6	7
2	3	4	5	6	7	8
3	4	5				
4	5					
5						
6						

2 How many totals are there altogether? ....

3 How many ways are there of making:

(a) 4? ....

(b) 6? ....

(c) 9? ....

(d) 12? ....

4 If $p(4) = \dfrac{\text{number of ways of making 4}}{\text{number of totals}}$

find:

(a) p(4) ....

(b) p(6) ....

(c) p(9) ....

(d) p(12) ....

5 What is the most likely score? ....

6 What is p(most likely score)? ....

7 Many board games start off by the participants having to throw a double 6. What other combination of two dice would have the same probability? ....

8 **(a)** What is the lowest possible total when three dice are thrown? ....

(b) What is the highest possible total? ....

(c) Find the probability of getting the highest total. ....

(d) How many ways could you get a total of 4 with three dice? ....

(e) Find the probability of getting a total of 4. ....

But does it all add up?

UNIT 8 Probability

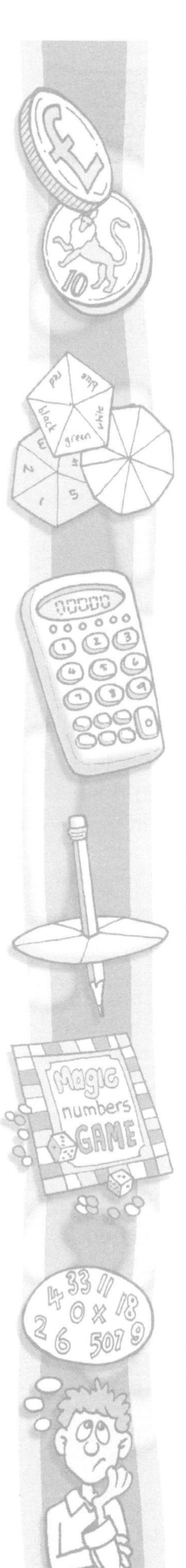

For three dice we would need a 3-dimensional table!
Rather than this we could *list* all the possible combinations.

For example, to make 5 we could have:

(2,2,1), (2,1,2), (1,2,2)
(3,1,1), (1,3,1), (1,1,3)

9 Complete the rows for a total of 6:

(4,1,1), (...,...,...), (...,...,...)
(3,2,1), (3,1,2), (1,...,...) (1,...,...), (2,...,...), (2,...,...)
(2,2,2)

10 What is p(total of 6)? ....

11 Complete the rows for a total of 9:

(6,2,1) (...,...,...), (...,...,...), (...,...,...), (...,...,...), (...,...,...)
(5,3,1) (...,...,...), (...,...,...), (...,...,...), (...,...,...), (...,...,...)
(5,2,2) (...,...,...), (...,...,...)
(4,4,1) (...,...,...), (...,...,...)
(4,3,2) (...,...,...), (...,...,...), (...,...,...), (...,...,...), (...,...,...)

12 What is p(total of 9)? ....

13 You are on your own for a total of 11!

14 What is p(total of 11)? ....

Throwing a die many times 1

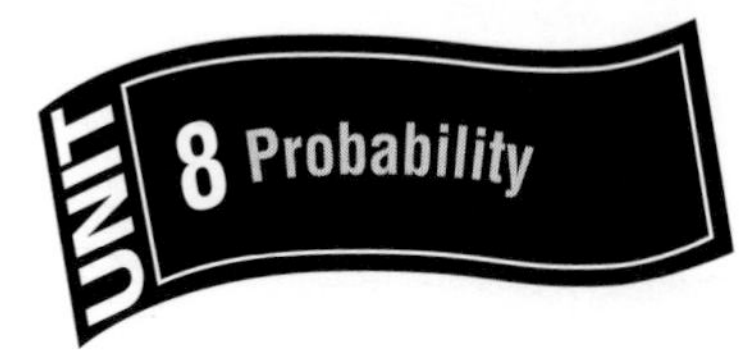

If you throw a die, each of the six sides has an equal chance of being on the top. So p(1) = $\frac{1}{6}$; p(2) = $\frac{1}{6}$, and so on.

If you throw a die 12 times, how many 1s would you expect to throw? You would expect to get 2.

Face on top	1	2	3	4	5	6
Number expected	2	2	2	2	2	2
My result						

Now throw your die 12 times and record your results in the row above.

Because you have thrown only a small number of times, your result may not be exactly the same as the 'Number expected' row. We really need to try lots of throws – 1200, for example! This would take a very long time and would be boring. We can use a computer or calculator to *simulate* throwing a die many times.

If your school has BBC or Archimedes computers you can use their BASIC programme. On the Archimedes, press F12. At the very bottom of the screen there will be a *. Type BASIC and press return. Then type in this programme carefully.

```
10 FOR N=1 TO 120
20 PRINT RND(6),
30 NEXT
```

Type RUN to start the programme.

This will print 120 random numbers (RND) between 1 and 6. You can then count up how many 1s, 2s, 3s, etc. and enter them on the table below. You also need to predict how many you should get (120 × $\frac{1}{6}$) of each.

Score	1	2	3	4	5	6
My experiment						
Prediction						

Although this is much quicker than throwing the die, you still have to add the number of each score. Add up all the totals in the second row above to make sure it comes to 120. It is very easy to miss a few!

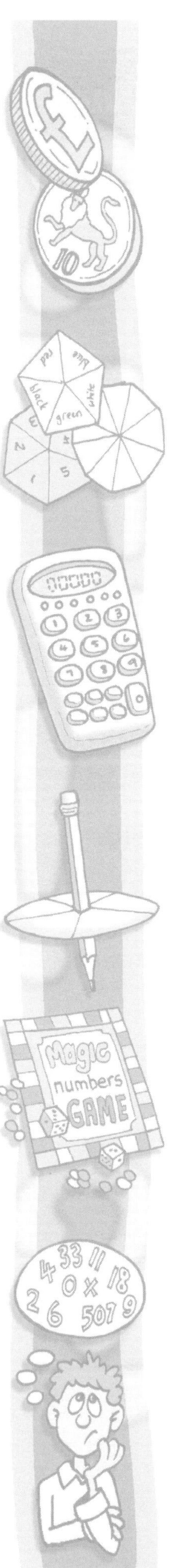

Throwing a die many times 1

We can change the programme to do the adding for us. In row 10, A, B, C, D, E and F are counters for the number of times that 1, 2, 3, 4, 5 and 6 occur.

Type the list out very carefully, using capital letters.

10 A=0: B=0: C=0: D=0: E=0: F=0	
20 FOR N=1 TO 120	
30 X=RND(6)	
40 IF X=1 THEN PROCONE	This takes us to line 200.
50 IF X=2 THEN PROCTWO	This takes us to line 300.
60 IF X=3 THEN PROCTHREE	This takes us to line 400.
70 IF X=4 THEN PROCFOUR	This takes us to line 500.
80 IF X=5 THEN PROCFIVE	This takes us to line 600.
90 IF X=6 THEN PROCSIX	This takes us to line 700.
100 NEXT	
110 PRINT A,B,C,D,E,F	This prints out the final totals of 1, 2, 3, 4, 5 and 6.
120 END	
200 DEFPROCONE 210 A=A+1 220 ENDPROC	This adds 1 to the total every time you throw a 1.
300 DEFPROCTWO 310 B=B+1 320 ENDPROC	This adds 1 to the total every time you throw a 2.
400 DEFPROCTHREE 410 C=C+1 420 ENDPROC	This adds 1 to the total every time you throw a 3.
500 DEFPROCFOUR 510 D=D+1 520 ENDPROC	This adds 1 to the total every time you throw a 4.
600 DEFPROCFIVE 610 E=E+1 620 ENDPROC	This adds 1 to the total every time you throw a 5.
700 DEFPROCSIX 710 F=F+1 720 ENDPROC	This adds 1 to the total every time you throw a 6.

Type RUN to start the programme.

Throwing a die many times 1

Run the programme a number of times. You will find that the totals are different because the machine is selecting random numbers each time.

You could change line 20 to change the number of throws.

Try: 10 FOR N=1 TO 1800 – this will simulate 1800 throws!

Complete the table below.

Score	1	2	3	4	5	6
Prediction number	300	300	300	300	300	300
Simulated score						

If you threw the die 1800 times and it took you 10 seconds per throw, how long would it take you? Then you have to add up the totals for each score! You can see why people use computers to simulate such activities.

Time how long it takes to run the programme with line 10=for n=1 to 18 000. How long would it take you at 10 seconds a throw?

If your school has PCs you will need to ask your teacher if it has BASIC.

Throwing a die many times 2
Using a spreadsheet

The school computers will have spreadsheets. This description is for Excel, but others should be similar.

Set up your Excel spreadsheet with the function =INT(RAND()*6)+1 where INT means integer (whole number) and RAND() is a random number equal to or greater than 0 and less than 1.

Pressing return gives the first random number in cell A1. To get further random numbers in the A column, drag the bottom right-hand corner of cell A1 downwards.

The picture on the right shows the 24 numbers generated. We need to group these as in the table below.

	A	B
1	1	
2	6	
3	3	
4	4	
5	3	
6	1	
7	4	
8	3	
9	6	
10	6	
11	4	
12	5	
13	2	
14	4	
15	6	
16	6	
17	4	
18	4	
19	4	
20	6	
21	3	
22	2	
23	6	
24	6	

Score	1	2	3	4	5	6
Spreadsheet						

Now try another 24 in column B. You will need to enter the formula =INT(RAND()*6)+1 in cell B1 and then drag the bottom right-hand corner down to B24.

Analyse your results and enter in the table above. What value would you *predict* should go in each column?

Now try a larger number of throws – you could do this by dragging the corner of B24 down to say B96. Analyse your results. (It is often useful to work in pairs so one can read out the entries in column B and the other can put the numbers in the correct column.)

Fill in your results in the table below. How close are they to your prediction for 96 ($96 \times \frac{1}{6}$)? Try another two columns and enter your results.

Score	1	2	3	4	5	6
Predict	16	16	16	16	16	16
Try 1						
Try 2						
Try 3						

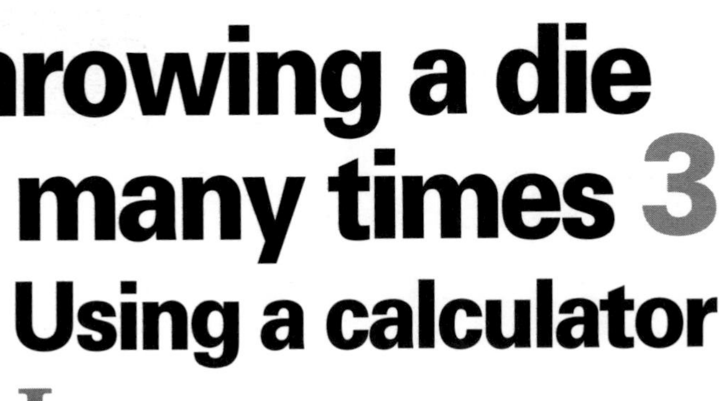

Throwing a die many times 3

Using a calculator

If you have a scientific calculator, there are usually two buttons in the bottom left-hand corner that can be used to generate **random numbers**.

The button we need is #RND. This generates a random number greater than or equal to 0 and less than 1. But we want whole numbers greater than or equal to 1 and less than or equal to 6. On the calculator, INT takes the integer (whole number) part of a decimal – for example INT(3.742)=3. We could do INT(#RND x 6), which would give us integers (whole numbers) from 0 to 5, so we need to add 1 each time, i.e. INT(#RND x 6) + 1.

Obviously a computer program (see the 'Throwing a die many times – 1 and 2' task sheets) will do more of the work for us. If your school has graphic calculators, it is possible to program them. Consult your teacher.

Tree diagrams 1
Starting a board game

1 A new board game has been produced. The rules state that players can start the game when they have thrown a head with a coin and a 6 with a die.

Complete the tree diagram to calculate the theoretical probabilities.

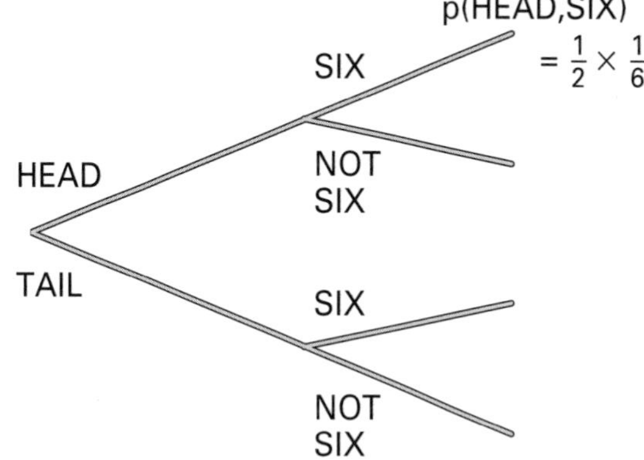

2 What is the probability of the player starting at the first attempt?

....

3 What is the probability of **not** starting at the first attempt?

....

4 What is the probability of a player starting at the **second** attempt?

....

Another game starts by having to throw three coins and getting at least two heads.

5 Complete the tree diagram.

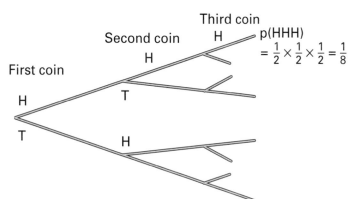

First coin
Second coin
Third coin

H — H — H p(HHH) $= \frac{1}{2} \times \frac{1}{2} \times \frac{1}{2} = \frac{1}{8}$

T

T — H

6 What is the probability of throwing at least two heads?

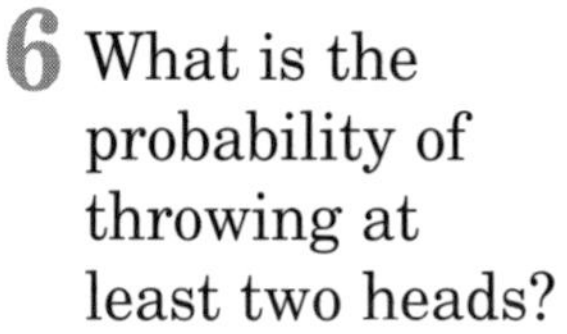

....

Use the same tree diagram for the following:

7 Find the probability of throwing at least one head. ....
(Try to use the easy way!)

Tree diagrams 2

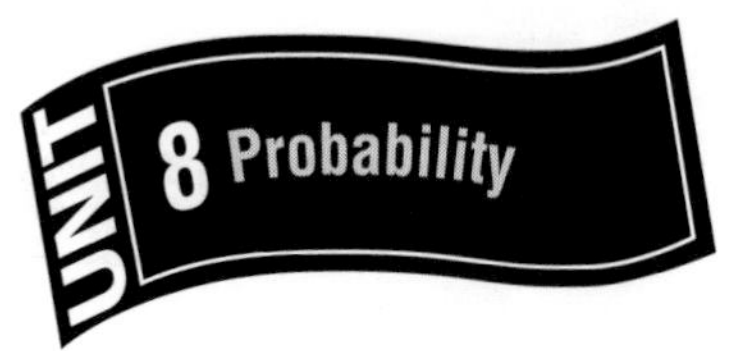

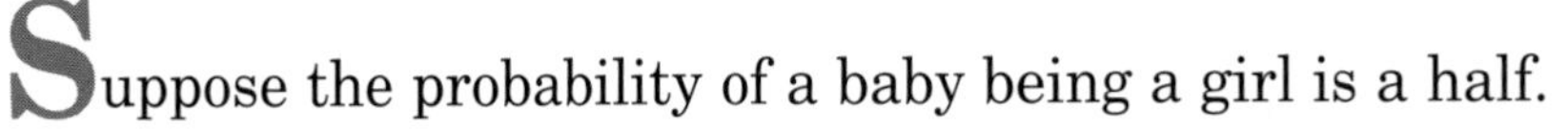
Suppose the probability of a baby being a girl is a half.

A family has three children. Complete the tree diagram to help you answer the questions that follow.

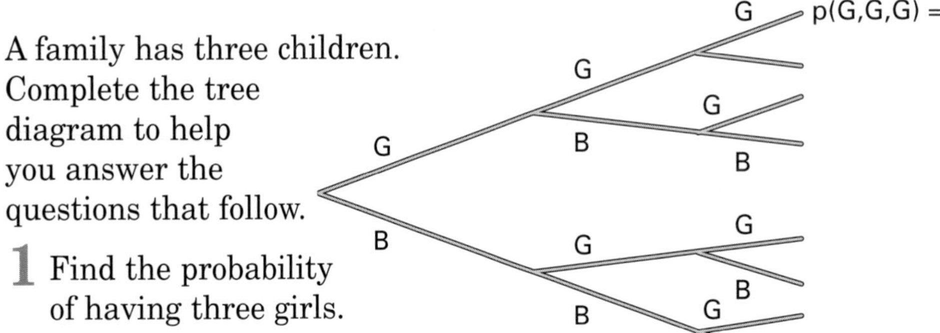

1 Find the probability of having three girls.

....

2 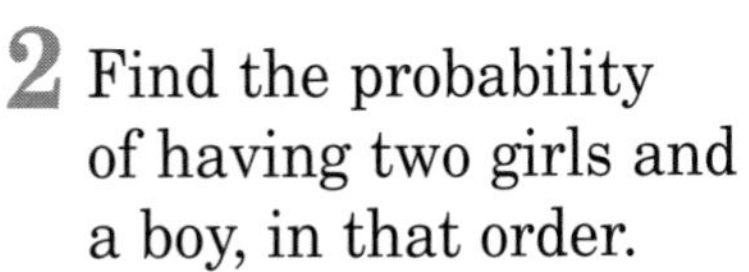
Find the probability of having two girls and a boy, in that order.

....

3 Find the probability of having two girls and a boy, in any order.

....

A family in the USA has 11 boys.

4 Find the probability of having 11 boys and no girls.

....

5 If that family had another child, what is the probability that it would be a girl?

....

The latest figures for childbirth show that more boys are born than girls. In 1996 in the UK there were 333 000 boy births and 316 000 girl births. Answer the following questions – you may find that a tree diagram helps.

6 What was the total number of births for 1996?

....

7 What percentage of the births were boys?

....

8 Using that figure, find the probability of a family with four children having:

(a) four boys ....

(b) four girls ....

(c) two boys and two girls, in that order ....

(d) two boys and two girls, in any order ....

(e) more girls than boys ....

Relative frequency

In an experiment, Daniel recorded the following scores from throwing a die 86 times:

6 3 3 4 2 5 5 5 1 4 6 2 5 3 3 6 1 3 3 6 4 3 4 2 6 5 4 4 2
1 4 1 5 3 2 4 2 4 6 5 1 2 1 3 5 3 2 2 5 4 2 1 3 2 2 3 4 6
3 5 5 2 3 1 4 2 6 5 4 4 4 3 1 2 2 1 2 2 5 5 2 5 3 6 5 6

He looked at the pattern of the 6s:

- The first 6 is the first score, so relative frequency is $\frac{1}{1} = 1$.
- The second 6 is the 11th score, so relative frequency is $\frac{2}{11} = 0.1218$.
- The third 6 is the 16th score, so relative frequency is $\frac{3}{16} = 0.1875$, and so on.

1 Complete Daniel's table below:

Number of 6s	1	2	3	4	5	6	7	8	9	10
Position	1	11	16	20	25	39	58	67	84	86
Relative frequency	1	0.1218	0.1875							

2 What would you predict that the relative frequency for throwing a 6 would be? ....

3 Use Daniel's data to investigate the pattern of 2s. Make a table similar to the one above. (Find out how many 2s there are in the data *before* you construct your table.)

4 In an experiment with throwing a die, Amy records the number of 1s like this:

Number of 1s	1	2	3	4	5	6	7	8	9	10
Number of throws	3	7	11	25	33	35	37	54	55	56
Relative frequency										

Number of 1s	11	12	13	14	15					
Number of throws	69	74	75	78	95					
Relative frequency										

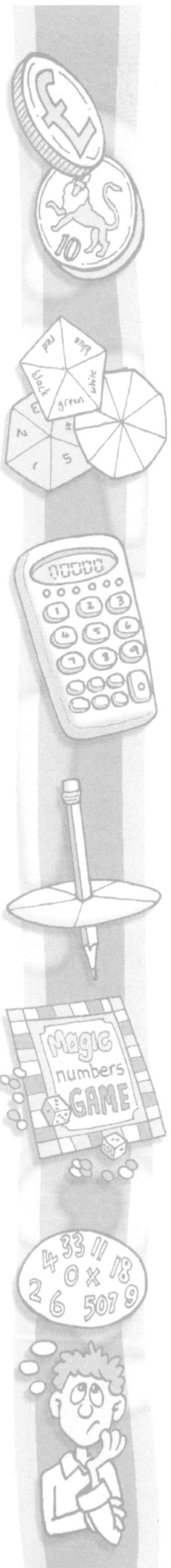

Relative frequency

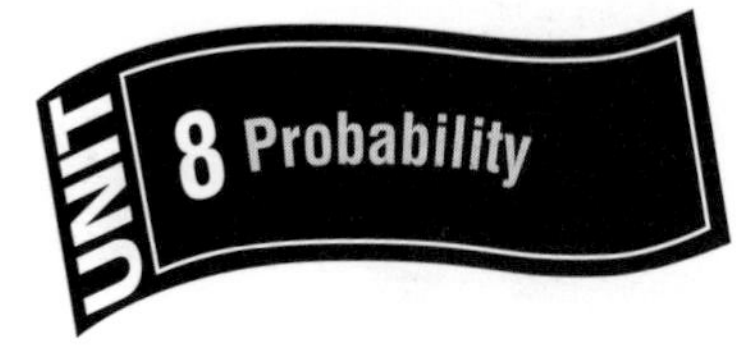

You could obtain data by a simple computer program:

```
10  A=0
20  FOR N=1 TO 180
30  X=RND(1)
40  IF X=6 THEN A=A+1
50  PRINT A;N
60  NEXT
70  END
```

A would provide the values for 'Number of 1s'.
N would provide values for 'Number of throws'.

How could you change the program to print the relative frequency?

If you have access to a suitable computer, type in the above program carefully and run it. Enter your results in the table below and work out the relative frequencies. (You could also do this on a spreadsheet.)

Number of 1s	1	2	3	4	5	6	7	8	9	10	11	12
Number of throws												
Relative frequency												

Number of 1s	13	14	15	16	17	18	19	20	21	22	23	24
Number of throws												
Relative frequency												

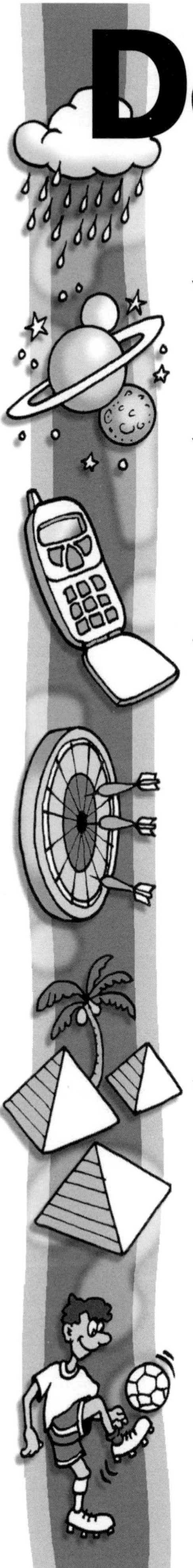

Dealing with data

Main focus

Interpreting and representing data in context

Content

Manipulating and representing data

Extracting and calculating numerical information from tables and graphs

Notes for teachers

The activities are designed to help pupils handle numbers in a range of contexts.

In order to make this experience more realistic, it is useful to start by discussing some examples of numerical information from books on subjects such as geography, history and science. Numerical information in newspapers or magazines is also a rich source for classroom discussion.

Learning outcomes

The pupils are able to:

- extract relevant data from given tables, graphs and literature;
- understand and apply mathematics to a wider context;
- handle large numbers;
- obtain approximate mental answers.

Evaluation

Could the pupils:

- extract appropriate data?
- decide on appropriate operations to solve problems?
- understand and use the facilities on a calculator appropriate to the tasks?
- offer solutions in the context of the problems in selecting an appropriate degree of accuracy?
- demonstrate appropriate problem-solving strategies?

Further activity

Ask pupils to bring examples of numerical data that they use in other subject areas, and discuss various approaches to tackling this.

Resources

Copies of pupil task sheets; books, magazines and newspapers with 'rich' numerical and graphical data

The planets

Below is a table of information about the planets. They revolve around the sun.

Planet	Radius of orbit around sun (million km)	Diameter of planet (km)	Orbit in days	Mass × Earth	Orbital speed (km/s)	Scale distance from the Sun (see question 7)
Mercury	58	4878	88	0.055	47.9	10 cm
Venus	108	12 103	225	0.815	35.0	18.6 cm
Earth	150	12 756	365.25	1	29.9	
Mars	228	6786	687	0.11	24.1	
Jupiter	778	142 980	4346	317.8	13.1	
Saturn	1427	120 548	10 776	95.2	9.7	
Uranus	2871	51 120	30 700	14.54	6.8	
Neptune	4497	49 536	60 225	17.2	5.4	
Pluto	5914	2200	90 520	0.002	4.7	

Look at the table and use it to answer these questions:

1 Which planet has the largest diameter? ....

2 Which planet has the smallest diameter? ....

3 How many times bigger is the largest than the smallest? ....

4 List the planets in order of their diameter (largest to smallest).

1 ....
2 ....
3 ....
4 ....
5 ....
6 ....
7 ....
8 ....
9 ....

5 List the planets in order of their mass (heaviest to lightest).

1 ....
2 ....
3 ....
4 ....
5 ....
6 ....
7 ....
8 ....
9 ....

The planets

6 Are the lists for questions 4 and 5 in the same order? Would you expect them to be?

....

You may need a calculator for the following questions.

To calculate the orbit of Mars in 'Earth years' we use:

687 ÷ 365.25 = 1.88 (2 dp)

7 Calculate the orbit of Jupiter in 'Earth years'.

....

To make a model of the Sun and the orbits of its planets, we could make the distance from the Sun to Mercury, its nearest planet, say 10 cm.

So the distance from the Sun to Venus will be (108 ÷ 58) × 10 = 18.6 cm.

8 Find the scale distances from the Sun to Earth, Mars and Jupiter.

Earth: ....
Mars: ....
Jupiter: ....

9 The planet furthest away from the Sun is Pluto. Find the scale distance to Pluto.

....

The model is getting large!

Where are the wettest places in the world?

The wettest inhabited place in the world is given as Buenaventura in Colombia, with an average annual rainfall of 6743 mm (265.27 inches). The driest place is Aswan in Egypt, with 0.5 mm (0.02 inches).

In the United Kingdom the wettest place is Dalness in Strathclyde, with a rainfall of 3306 mm (130.16 inches).

1 Find the annual rainfall in your area and add your result to the table below.

Place	Country	Average rainfall
Buenaventura	Colombia	6743 mm
Aswan	Egypt	0.05 mm
Dalness	Scotland	3306 mm
My area		

2 Make a horizontal bar graph of the information given here. Use the scales given below.

Rainfall (mm)

Place	0	1000	2000	3000	4000	5000	6000	7000
Buenaventura								
Dalness								
My area								
Aswan								

Age pyramids

The table below shows the age distribution of males and females in the UK and Brazil in 1991, given in percentages of the total population of each country.

Age band	UK male	UK female	Brazil male	Brazil female
0–4	3.4	3.3	5.7	6.4
5–9	3.3	3.1	5.9	5.9
10–14	3.1	2.9	5.4	5.4
15–19	3.5	3.3	4.9	4.9
20–24	4.0	3.9	4.6	4.6
25–29	4.2	4.1	4.5	4.5
30–34	3.6	3.5	3.8	3.8
35–39	3.3	3.3	3.2	3.2
40–44	3.6	3.6	2.6	2.6
45–49	3.0	3.0	2.0	2.0
50–54	2.7	2.7	1.7	1.8
55–59	2.5	2.6	1.4	1.5
60–64	2.4	2.6	1.2	1.2
65–69	2.3	2.7	0.9	1.0
70–74	1.6	2.2	0.6	0.7
75–79	1.3	2.0	0.4	0.5
80–84	0.7	1.4	0	0
85+	0.4	1.1	0	0

We can get a better understanding of this data if we make age pyramids. The one for the UK has been partially drawn. Complete it and then do the one for Brazil.

Age pyramid for the United Kingdom

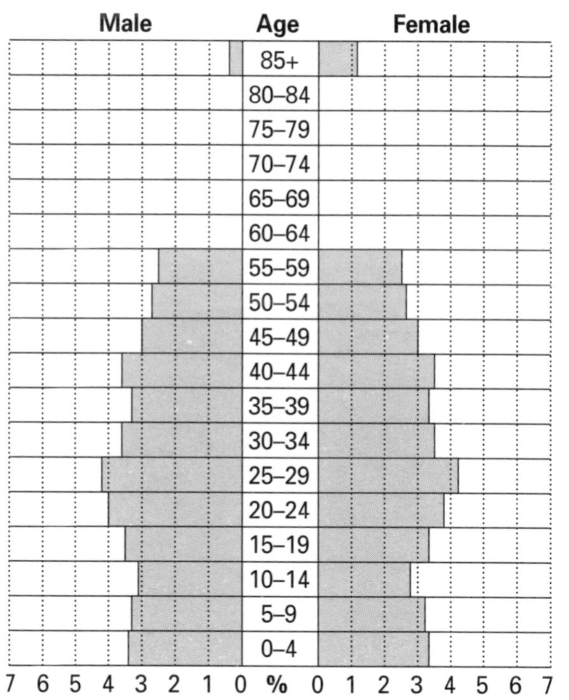

Age pyramid for Brazil

Male	Age	Female
	85+	
	80–84	
	75–79	
	70–74	
	65–69	
	60–64	
	55–59	
	50–54	
	45–49	
	40–44	
	35–39	
	30–34	
	25–29	
	20–24	
	15–19	
	10–14	
	5–9	
	0–4	
7 6 5 4 3 2 1 0	%	0 1 2 3 4 5 6 7

Age pyramids

Look at the two pyramids and the table data to answer these questions:

1 What percentage of Brazilians are aged under 25? ....

2 What percentage of UK citizens are aged under 25? ....

3 What percentage of Brazilians are aged 70 or over? ....

4 What percentage of UK citizens are aged 70 or over? ....

5 Darren said that there are always more men than women in the UK. At what age does this cease to be true? ....

6 Look at the ages from 70 onwards in both countries. Give at least two differences and describe them.

....

....

....

7 The total population of Brazil is 150 367 000.
Approximately how many Brazilians are aged 15–19? ....

8 The total population of the UK is 57 410 600.
Approximately how many of them are aged 15–19? ....

9 A friend rings up and has not done the age pyramids for homework. Describe them to her as though over the phone, bringing out any differences and similarities.

....

....

....

....

....

....

10 Explain why you think that the UK and Brazil were chosen for this exercise.

....

....

....

Some world statistics

The table below gives statistics for 24 countries. Although there are many more countries than this in the world, the table does include those with the largest populations, largest areas and largest and smallest population densities (people per square mile). Population density is found by dividing the population by the area in square miles.

Country	Population	Area (square miles)	Population density
UK	58 919 000	94 251	625
France	56 616 000	210 026	
Germany	82 143 000	137 830	
Spain	39 323 000	195 364	
New Zealand	3 653 000	104 454	
Australia	18 508 000	2 966 200	
USA	267 839 000	3 679 192	
Singapore	3 104 000	249	
The Netherlands	15 619 000	16 033	
Egypt	62 110 000	385 229	
Hong Kong	6 491 000	415	
Monaco	31 900	0.75	
Iceland	271 000	39 699	
Jamaica	2 536 000	4 244	
India	967 613 000	1 222 243	
China	1 227 740 000	3 696 100	
Russia	147 231 000	6 592 800	
Pakistan	136 183 000	307 374	
Brazil	159 691 000	3 300 171	
Japan	126 110 000	145 877	
Canada	30 287 000	3 849 674	
Denmark	5 284 000	16 639	
Macau	421 000	8.1	
South Africa	42 446 000	470 693	

Some world statistics

Look at the table and then answer the following questions:

1 Which are the three biggest countries in the world in terms of area?
1.. 2.. 3..

2 Which three countries have the largest population?
1.. 2.. 3..

3 Complete the population density column, giving your answers to the nearest person.

4 Which three countries have the largest population density?
1.. 2.. 3..

5 Which three countries have the smallest population density?
1.. 2.. 3..

League tables

UNIT 9 Dealing with data

After playing ten football matches, the number of points scored by Manchester United is 26. Three points are given for a win, 1 point for a draw and of course no points for a defeat.

1 Complete this row of the Premier League Table:

Team	Played	Won	Drew	Lost	Points
Manchester United	10				26

2 Southampton have 20 points. Suppose they have not lost any games. Fill in the missing details:

Team	Played	Won	Drew	Lost	Points
Southampton	10				20

3 Suppose they had lost at least one game. Fill in the missing details:

Team	Played	Won	Drew	Lost	Points
Southampton	10				20

4 Chelsea have 24 points. Give two possible ways of making the 24 points. Fill in the details below:

Team	Played	Won	Drew	Lost	Points
Chelsea	10				24
Chelsea	10				24

Rugby union

In rugby union you score 5 points for a try, 2 points for a conversion and 3 points for a penalty. You only take a conversion after a try is scored, so the number of conversions must be equal to or less than the number of tries.

5 In a recent match, Sale scored 23 points and Bath 19 points. Investigate how each score could be made up. If there is more than one way, list them all.

....

....

....

League tables

6 Are there any totals that are impossible to make in rugby? (One is an obvious answer!) List any that you find, up to a score of 50.

....

....

....

7 Can you think of a systematic way of tackling this problem to ensure that you had not missed any? Explain your method.

....

....

....

Rugby league

In a recent game, Halifax beat Castleford by 29 points to 16. We know that Halifax scored five tries, four penalty goals and a dropped goal (worth 1 point), and that Castleford scored two tries and four penalty goals.

8 From the above information, work out how many points are awarded for a try and how many for a penalty. Show your reasoning.

....

....

....

9 One pupil said that, unlike rugby union, any score is possible in rugby league (see question 6). Is she correct? Give your reasons.

....

....

....

....

....

Winning at darts

In darts, the board has numbers 1 to 20 with each number having doubles and trebles; 25 points are given for an inner bull's eye and 50 points for an outer bull (an outer bull counts as a double).

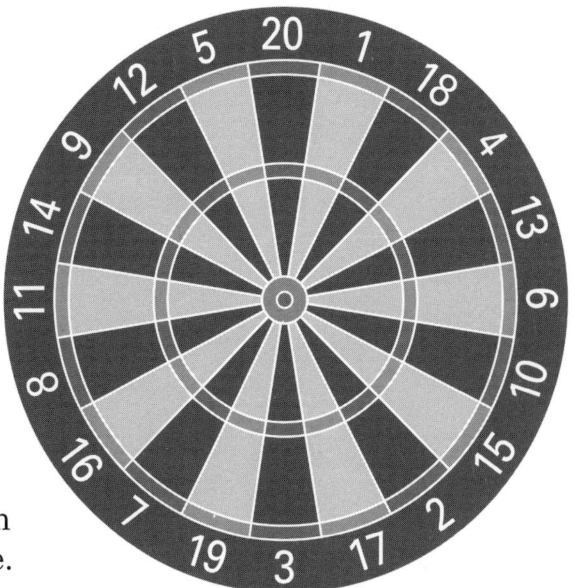

The player starts off with a score of 301 or 501 and, in order to win, has to reduce this to zero before their opponent does. The players each have three darts. They take it in turns to throw and reduce their score.

For example, a player needs 93 to win, with three darts to throw. To win, the final throw must be a double and the score must be exactly equal to 93. One way would be treble 20 (60); that leaves 33. The third throw has to be a double, which will be an even number, so the second throw must be an odd number. One solution would be: treble 20, 17, double 8. Another might be: treble 20, 1, double 16. If the player goes over 93, they go back to the score of 93 and lose the right to throw any remaining darts until the opponent has had their turn. The experts might take this into account in deciding which of the above ways to choose.

1 Explain how you could make up a score of 127 with three or fewer darts. Is there another way?

....

....

2 Describe how you would make the following final scores. If there are a number of different ways of making the total, list as many as you can.

(a) 101: ....

....

(b) 56: ....

....

(c) 79: ....

....

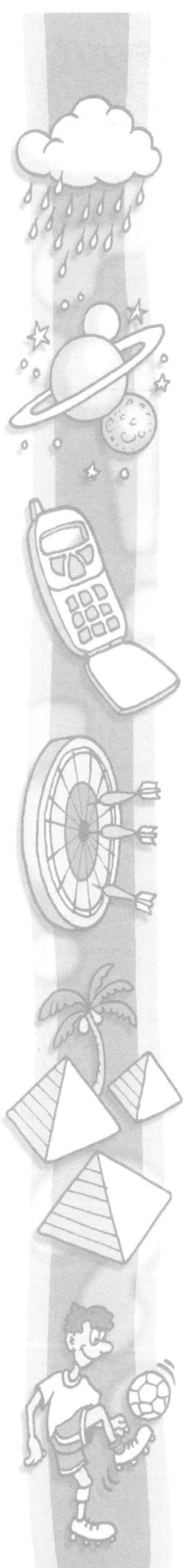

Winning at darts

(d) 93: ....

....

(e) 121: ....

....

3 Suppose someone got a final score of 97 with two darts.

(a) Explain why the player did not go for treble 20 with their first throw.

....

....

(b) Explain why there is only one possible way of getting this score with two darts.

....

....

(c) What is the only way?

....

4 Describe how you would make the following final scores with two darts only – if it is possible. If there is more than one way, give some examples.

(a) 93: ....

....

(b) 63: ....

....

(c) 110: ....

....

(d) 120: ....

....

(e) 33: ....

....

5 What is the maximum score that can be made with three darts? Explain how you would make it.

....

....

Winning at darts

6 Look at the order in which the numbers are placed around the dartboard:

20, 1, 18, 4, 13, 6, 10, 15, 2, 17, 3, 19, 7, 16, 8, 11, 14, 9, 12, 5

Can you suggest a reason why they are in this order? Explain this.

....

....

7 If you watch darts on TV you will notice that the expert players go for treble 20 in order to get high totals. What is the danger of this strategy for someone who is not an expert? Can you suggest a number to aim at which would help the non-expert to get a high score without too much risk of a very low score? Give reasons and examples.

....

....

....

....

....

How much does it cost to buy a house?

UNIT 9 Dealing with data

If you borrow money to buy a house you have to pay it back with interest – say 8.7%. The monthly repayment includes a certain amount of interest. The interest rate can change over time, of course.

If a family were taking out a mortgage now and wanted to borrow £45 000, this table from a bank shows their repayments over different periods of time.

Term (how many years)	Number of monthly repayments	Monthly amount (gross)	Total repaid	Amount paid in interest (Total = £45 000)
25 years	300	£368.44		
20 years	240	£396.24		
15 years	180	£448.42		

1 Complete the 'Total repaid' and the 'Amount paid in interest' columns.

2 Calculate 8.7% of £45 000 in 1 year. ....

3 Calculate 8.7% of £45 000 in:

(a) 25 years .... **(b)** 20 years .... **(c)** 15 years ....

4 Do the answers for question 3 agree with the figures in the 'Amount paid in interest' column? ....

5 Look at the very first monthly repayment for a 25-year mortgage. How much interest is paid in the first month? ....

6 If you take the interest away from the monthly repayment, how much of the loan have you paid back? ....

7 How much of the £45 000 still has to be paid back? ....

8 This is the amount you owe at the start of the second month. Calculate the interest to be paid on this for the second month. Is it the same or less than the interest you paid for the first month? ....

9 Can you see how the answers to questions 6, 7 and 8 can explain your answer to question 4? Say why.

....

....

....

Mobile phone charges

Before buying a mobile phone, people need to analyse how much and when they would use it. This helps decide which package to subscribe to because 'deals' vary so much.

- Peak or 'not peak' – that is the first question! (*Note*: 'peak time' is from 7am to 7pm Monday to Friday)
- Monthly subscription or 'Pay as you talk'?

	Monthly subscription	Charges per day	Standard talk time included (per month)	Standard calls (per minute)		Calls to other UK mobile networks		Text Messaging (per message)
				peak	off-peak	peak	off-peak	
Daily 50	n/a	50p	50 min off-peak per day	35p	1p	40p	25p	10p
All-time 20	£15.99	n/a	20 min	10p	10p	35p	35p	10p
Chat 60	£17.50	n/a	60 min	15p	5p	30p	12p	10p
Chat 120	£25.00	n/a	120 min	15p	5p	30p	12p	10p

Ros

I am at school all day where phones have been banned. I phone my friend every evening to chat and discuss our homework. I think I would use it for an hour every day after 7 pm.

Ali

I am a busy working mother. I have to travel 35 miles by train every day. I have to use my phone in the daytime to be in touch with my office, my husband and child minder. I think I would use it for an hour every weekday before 7 pm.

1 Both these people have chosen to use the same network whose charges are detailed in the table above. Choose the scheme that would be best for each of them. Make sure that you give enough evidence to show that it is the best option.

2 Some people do not use their phones to talk much every day but like sending lots of text messages. Another option could be to consider 'Pay as you talk'. There is no monthly line rental and the phone can be recharged with vouchers of different values.

Consider the two offers on the next page.

Mobile phone charges

A new type of phone tariff is called 'Pay as you talk'. There is no monthly line rental but the phone can be recharged with £15 of talk time. There is a choice of two ways of using the £15:

	Type 1	Type 2
First 3 minute (per day)	25p	25p
After 3 minutes (per day)	5p	5p
Sending text messages (per message)	10p	12p for first 3 messages each day 9p thereafter

3 Which is the best option to choose?
(a) Could you justify when it would be better to choose Type 1?
(b) Could you justify when it would be better to choose Type 2?

4 (a) Paul has the Type 1 option. He has used exactly £5 worth of units. He has used up his first 3 minutes of calls for 4 days and has sent 7 text messages. How many minutes did he use at the 5p rate?

(b) Paula has the Type 2 option. She has also used exactly £5 worth of units. She has used 10 minutes of time at the 'first 3 minutes of the day' rate and has sent 14 text messages at the 'first messages of the day' rate and 8 messages at the lower cost. For how many minutes did she use her phone at the lower phone rate?

5 Would YOU want the following deal? Give your reasons saying in what circumstances it would/would not be a good deal.

Type 1 Special Deal

For a one-off payment of £14.99 you have:

- 5 free text messages every day when your talk time is in credit
- an extra £5 of talk time
- two 30-second reserve calls when your talk time has run out

BUT YOU HAVE TO BUY YOUR PHONE FIRST AT ONLY £29.99!

Getting on the Internet

To connect your computer to the Internet you need a modem (this joins your machine to the telephone line) and a 'service provider', to whom you pay a rental each month.

There are different ways of paying for this service:

A A fixed charge, no matter how long you spend on the Internet.
e.g. Company A charges £11.75 per calendar month for unlimited time.

B A smaller charge for a limited number of hours per month, with an hourly charge for extra hours. e.g. Company B charges £6.50 a calendar month for up to 5 hours per month. Extra hours cost £1.95 per hour.

1 Find the break-even point for the two services, i.e. how many extra hours you can spend on Company B's rates before it becomes as expensive as Company A. ....

C Company C offers the following package: £25 set-up fee, then £10 per month unlimited time.

2 Which is cheaper in the first year, Company A or Company C? What about the second year? ....

....

D Some companies offer cheaper rates if you pay for the whole year in advance instead of monthly. e.g. Company D charges £14.69 monthly or £141 for the whole year.

3 How much money do you save? ....

4 Express this as a percentage of the normal method of paying. ....

5 The advantage is that you save money.
Can you think of at least two disadvantages? ....

....

6 Company A has an annual saver too – £11.75 per calendar month or £129.75 per year. What is the percentage saving on this? ....

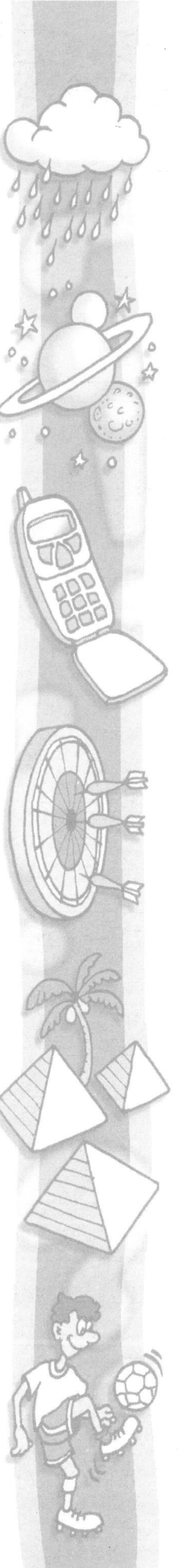

Getting on the Internet

E Company E has an annual payment of £70.50 for 5 hours per month, with extra hours charged at £2.06 per hour.

7 Assuming an average of 10 hours per month, what will the total annual cost be? ....

8 Compare this with the same amount of time for Company B (no annual fee here) and with the annual fee for Company A. What would be your bargain offer? ....

Remember you also have to pay for telephone charges!